# Along the Allegheny
## 2nd Edition

A History of the Early Events Along the
Allegheny and Its Tributaries

by

William Garbarino

Midway Publishing
P.O. Box 313
Midway, Pa 15060

Printed by
Closson Press
257 Delilah St, Apollo, PA 15613-1933
Published by
Midway Publishing
PO Box 313, Midway, PA 15060
ISBN #0967101417
Library of Congress Card Number 00-100719
Second Edition, February 2005

# ALONG THE ALLEGHENY

# CONTENTS

ALONG THE ALLEGHENY

## LIST OF ILLUSTRATIONS

# Acknowledgements

When I was a young boy growing up in Kersey, occasionally my grandfather, Frederick Dollinger, would tell me stories about what the area was like in by-gone years. He once told me that the hill, on which his house sat, was a divide. He told me how this impacted the early logging industry in the area. All the water on one side ran to Pittsburgh and all the water on the other side ran to Williamsport. Therefore, all the timber cut on one side of the divide was rafted to Pittsburgh and all the timber cut on the other side of the divide was rafted to Williamsport.

I chose the development along the Allegheny River as a topic for a term paper, while working on a Master of Arts Degree with California State University. While working on the paper, I became so interested in the Early History of Western Pennsylvania, that I began reading everything that I could find on the subject and decided that someone should tell these stories to the public.

I would like to acknowledge the many fine scholars of Pennsylvania History who have scrupulously recorded the events that I have included in this book. Without their research and documentation, I would not have been able to assemble this book and tell the stories of the Allegheny River. I would also like to acknowledge the Carnegie Library of Pittsburgh for use of its outstanding Pennsylvania Room, and the West Allegheny Library for its support in obtaining the research materials that I needed to complete this book.

Since the popularity of this book has grown, a second printing was needed which has provided me an opportunity to make some editorial changes and add some additional illustrations, resulting in a second edition.

WILLIAM M. GARBARINO, JR.

# Introduction

The Allegheny is frequently referred to in early writings as the "Ohio". The name Ohio is derived from the Indian term "O-hee-yo" that means "Beautiful River," or as later called by the French "La Belle Riviere." The Allegheny River Valley (watershed) has been the scene of many historical events which have had a significant amount of influence on the expansion of American civilization as we know it. The struggles and trials presented to those who fought to inhabit the area had an indelible impact on the development of the American character. The early American settlers tried, and were successful, in taming the wilderness. However, their efforts were confronted by a people who valued the wilderness as it was, and they were determined to fight over their "Alleghenny." The Indians saw the Allegheny Valley as home and provider of all the things they needed. The agrarian culture of Western Europe came into direct conflict with that of the inhabitants who practiced hoe culture and were hunter-gatherers. The conflict resulted in a struggle among the Indians in 1649 over furs. It ended with the eventual capitulation of the Valley by the Indians to the Americans in 1795.

Following the Treaty of Greenville (Ohio), the newly established Americans came in great numbers to the Allegheny Valley, and soon found the river to be its greatest resource. The river and its tributaries lay at the economic heart of the valley. Its flowing waters provided the needed transportation for people and goods traveling up and down western Pennsylvania and New York. It became the key highway for distribution of needed goods to people living along its shores as well as those of the Ohio and the Great Lakes. The river played a critical role in the War of 1812, ferrying materials to Commodore Perry on Lake Erie for the construction of his small fleet. It was the source of transportation for migrants, timber, agricultural products, salt, and other raw materials. Along its shores all types of vessels have been built from dugouts to war ships. Many communities, such as Kittanning and Warren, which had their origins as Indian villages, blossomed into cities booming with economic opportunities. The Allegheny is appropriately called the "Beautiful River."

**Along the Allegheny**

# Early Inhabitants

Pennsylvania has been inhabited for at least thirteen thousand years or more. Archeological evidence has placed the age of artifacts found at Meadowcroft to be between thirteen and twenty thousand years old. This conflicts with the popularly held belief that man only entered Pennsylvania during the late glacial period.

About ten thousand BC, bands of hunting-gathering people known as Archaics were inhabiting Pennsylvania. Barry C. Kent describes the shelters at the sites that have been found as follows: "Those few sites that have been discovered suggest circular, dome shaped, bark covered frameworks of poles. When travelling or in temporary hunting camps, Archaic folk generally made use of natural shelters such as rock overhangs." He indicates that the Archaics lived in bands of twenty five to fifty people and occupied territories defined by drainage areas such as streams and tributaries. The Archaics existed until about one thousand BC[1]

Following the Archaics came another group of people commonly found along our rivers and streams. These "Transitional" people relied more heavily upon the rivers for subsistence than did the previous Archaic people. They were known by there broad, well flaked spear points and their original use of vessels for cooking. Previously all cooking had been done over the open fire or by baking.[2]

The best known of the early inhabitants of the Allegheny River Valley were members of the "Mound Builders." The Mound Builders flourished through out the Ohio River Valley. They got their name from building large burial and ceremonial mounds. The earliest of these mound building societies is known as the Adena who lived in the area between 500 BC and 200 AD  The Adena were also known for manufacturing highly crafted tools and ornaments out of stones and copper.  They were replaced by the Hopewell people, also mound builders, from 100 BC to 350 AD[3]  The mounds located on the upper Allegheny give evidence to the Hopewell Indians, while the mounds along the lower Allegheny closer to Pittsburgh, have been influenced by the Adena.  The mounds near Pittsburgh are referred to as the Oakmont and Darlington mounds.  The mounds on the upper Allegheny are known as the Irvine Mound Group (near the mouth of Brokenstraw Creek), the Cornplanter Mound Group (east of the mouth of Cornplanter Run), the Corydon mounds (one quarter mile east of the Allegheny River), and the Sugar Run Group (near Kinzua). [4]

**Transitional Period Spearpoint**

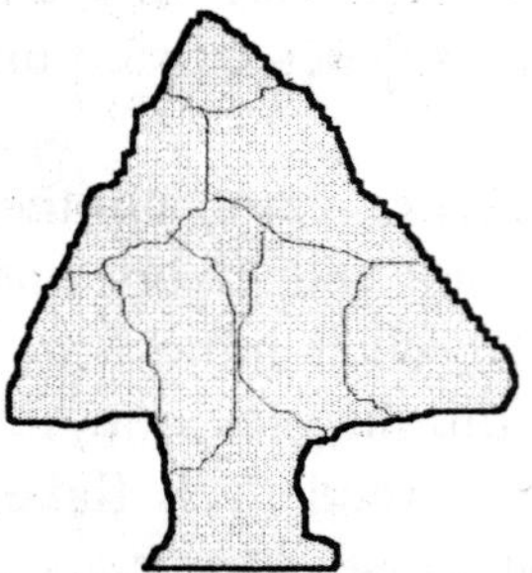

As to be expected evidence of the Indians following the Hopewells abounds throughout western Pennsylvania and western New York.  "The History of Cataraugus County, New York" provides many examples of prehistoric fortifications and other sites occupied by prehistoric people.  The fortifications described are usually in the shape of an irregular circle between two hundred to three hundred and forty feet in diameter. They include an earthen parapet approximately three feet high accompanied by a ditch on the outside about three feet deep. Inside these fortifications many arrow heads have been found along ancient hearths, and pits used for storage as well as refuse. Most of these fortifications are located on high ground or an easily defended location. However this is not always the case.[5]

Later, we find groups of Indians referred to as the Monongahela, McFate, and Owasco groups populating the Allegheny River Valley. The Monongahela people lived in the lower end of the Allegheny from the Kiskiminetas River south to northern West Virginia and Maryland, and southeastern Ohio. Generally speaking, they lived in Southwestern Pennsylvania. They got their name from the many archeological sites found along the Monongahela River. The Monongahela people lived in the area as late as the beginning of the Historic Period, or the beginning the 17th Century. By 1550 European goods had reached these Indians through trade with Indians of the upper Allegheny area. The Monongahela people were agrarians growing corn, pumpkins, beans, and tobacco. They supplemented their diet by hunting and gathering. Their settlements usually include a circular palisaded fort with huts near the interior side of the palisaded wall. The huts were made of saplings covered with hides, bark, or woven mats. They were twenty feet in diameter and had storage pits located near them.[6]

# Along the Allegheny

## Palisaded Fort

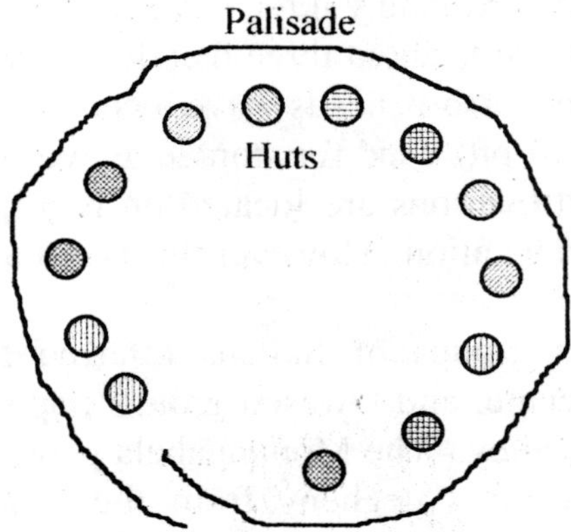


The McFate Indians were a nomadic group of Indians who lived in the upper regions of the Allegheny Valley from 1450 AD to 1600 AD. The name McFate comes from the original site were evidence of these people was found, which was on the McFate property in Crawford County. There original tribal name is unknown. According to archaeologist Andrew J Myer[7], the artifacts discovered indicate that they were closely related to Iroquoin culture. The territory ranged from Crawford county in the west to Clinton county in Central Pennsylvania, and from Cattaraugus and Chautauqua counties in New York to Armstrong county in Southwestern Pennsylvania. A distinguishing factor of McFate culture is "incised" pottery.

The ancestors of the McFate's were the Mound Builders (Hopewell) previously mentioned. According to Myers they were living along the Allegheny River between AD 500 and 900, and along the Mahoning and Beaver Rivers and the glacial swamps and lakes of western Pennsylvania. In the early 1400's the McFate's moved to the Kinzua area on the upper reaches of the Allegheny River where they lived at peace with other Indians in the area. About 1430, they moved again, possibly because of the effect the "Little Ice Age" had on their ability to raise crops. We find them again from 1450 through 1580 living on the Allegheny Plateau at such places as French Creek Valley and Chautauqua and Cattaraugus counties in New York. Evidence of their settlements can be found in the remnants of their palisaded villages located on hill tops, in caves, and at spring heads. Between 1580 and 1600, they migrated south taking up residence with the Monongahela People. A confederacy was formed between themselves and other tribes but appears they all fell victim to the mighty Iroquois. The McFate's disappeared prior to making contact with Europeans and no written record exists of these people.

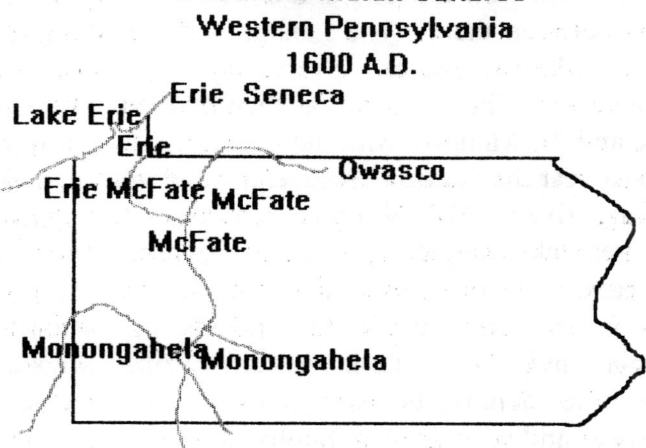


The Owasco culture was centered in New York but some villages have been found in northern Pennsylvania.

Archaeologists believe these people were the forefathers of the Iroquoian Culture first encountered by the white man. They resided in Northern Pennsylvania from Ohio to New York between 1000 AD and 1300 AD.

According to Indian legend, the banks of the Allegheny River were originally inhabited by the Alleghans (Allegewi). The term Allegheny is considered by some to have been derived from the Indian term Alligewi-hanna (Stream of the Allegewi) or Alligewi-sipu (River of the Allegewi).[8] They preceded the Lenni Lenape (Delaware) and the Mengwe (Iroquois).

The legend continues: The Algonquian speaking Lenape migrated from west of the Mississippi River all the way to the east coast. During this process they joined with the Mengwe who were also migrating eastward. The Allegewi, seeing the great numbers of the combined tribes entering their territory east of the Mississippi, resisted this encroachment into their territory and a war was waged for many years between them. The Lenape and the Mengwe defeated the Allegewi and drove them out and down the Mississippi valley. The territory was then divided between the Lenape and the Mengwe with the Lenape settling along the east coast near the Hudson, Susquehanna, Potomac, and the Delaware rivers. The Mengwe settled in the north below the great lakes and along the Saint Lawrence River.[9]

The Lenape were prosperous and became increasingly influential in the area, while the Indians in northern Pennsylvania and New York were warring among themselves. The Mengwe became jealous of the Lenape's growing power and with great difficulty among themselves formed the confederacy known as the Five Nations. This confederacy, which was comprised of the Mohawk (Man Eaters), Oneida (Standing Rock), Onondagas (On top of the

Hill), Cayugas (The Place Where Locusts Were Taken Out), and the Seneca (Mountaineers), was formed between 1400 and 1600 to provide a common defense against the Lenape and other tribes in the area.[10] These Indians all spoke languages within the Iroquoian Language Group. The confederacy became known as the Iroquois Confederacy. Iroquois is a French corruption of the Algonquian term which meant "Real Adders." The Iroquois refer to themselves as the Kanonsionni which means "People of the Long House."

The legendary leaders of the development of the Confederacy are known as Hiawatha (Onondaga) and Deganawida (Wendat or Huron). Both men had been victims of their desire for peace. Hiawatha had suffered the death of three daughters, one death each time he held council with the other tribes to establish peace among them. Deganawida had been scorned into leaving his village because of his ideas. Deganawida (Peacemaker) and Hiawatha found refuge in a Mohawk village where they joined forces to establish peace among the tribes from which the Iroquois Confederacy evolved.[11]

The symbol of this peace was a tall White Pine with an eagle at its crest and white roots at its base. "The Tree of Peace was seen as a great white pine 'rising to meet the sun' (the Eye of the Creator), with branches representing the law and white (i.e. living) roots extending to the Four Quarters of the earth so that men everywhere might be able to trace peace to its source. Above the tree was the Eagle That Sees Afar, symbol of 'preparedness,' watching the horizon to warn peace-loving people of approaching danger."[12] Anyone who followed the roots to the Tree of Peace could live under the protection of the Iroquois Confederacy.

Delaware is an English term given to the Lenni Lenape. It is derived from their early association with the Delaware River, which had been named after Lord De La Warr. The Lenape (Delaware), an Algonquian speaking people, comprised of the Munsee (Wolf), Unami (Turtle), Unalachtigo (Turkey), were defeated between 1609 and 1620 by the Iroquois leaving the Five Nations the most powerful nation in the east.

## The Tree of Peace

# The Struggle for the Allegheny

The Iroquois and the Delaware nations were agrarian, practicing Hoe Culture, prior to the arrival of the Europeans. They raised corn and other crops and supplemented them with hunting for game, foraging for edible plants, fruits, and nuts, as well as fishing. Depending upon the season, they traveled to favorite hunting or fishing grounds. By 1649 the Indians had been in contact with the Europeans for almost one hundred years, first the Dutch, then the French, and later the English. They quickly adopted the implements, technology, and materials of the Europeans to include; log cabins, cloth, needles, flour, iron kettles for cooking, iron tools for wood working and cultivation, traps, guns, gun powder and ball. In order to obtain these items the Indians traded furs. This required a much larger hunting area than required to catch and kill game to feed themselves and their families. The negative side of trading furs for goods was that many of the Indians had given up their primitive ways of hunting and trapping for food and clothing. The Beaver now bought everything they needed and they became economically dependent on trading with these foreigners for their survival.

By 1649 the economic dependence of the Iroquois on the French for material goods led to the Beaver Wars. The hunting grounds of the Iroquois had been "hunted out" and their neighbors, with the encouragement of the French, would not share their hunting grounds with them. This impasse became a matter of survival for the Iroquois and they began a series of wars called the "Beaver Wars". They invaded the Allegheny and upper Ohio River Basin annihilating or dispersing the Erie and other minor tribes in the area.

# Along the Allegheny

"So great was the scourge of the Iroquois that, during the closing decades of the 17th Century and the first two decades of the 18th Century, the region south of Lake Erie on both sides of the Allegheny and upper Ohio rivers contained practically no Indian population and the Iroquois looked upon this vast territory as their great hunting ground." [13]

Much of the struggle between the Iroquois and the Eries (Cat People) took place along the Allegheny River. There were numerous excursions against one another of mortal combat. J. S. Schenck and W. S. Rank in The History of Warren County, PA state that there were several times when the Erie attacked the Iroquois but were driven back. On one occasion several hundred Iroquois attacked a force of Erie, three times their size, and killed or dispersed them. This battle is believed to have taken place fourteen miles below Brokenstraw and has been referred to as the "Burying Ground". Another battle was fought on the upper waters of the Allegheny River in Cattaraugus County, NY resulting in another enormous loss to the Eries. [14] In 1648, the Dutch, had provided the Iroquois with over four hundred muskets which contributed to their success in warfare. [15] However, the most dramatic reduction in the Erie population is believed to have been caused by disease, possibly measles, or small pox.

This invasion, driven by the demand for furs in Europe and the need for the Iroquois to maintain the necessities of life, marked a dramatic departure from the economic use of the Allegheny Valley for subsistence hunting and fishing. The Allegheny River Valley was now being valued as a vital economic resource. It provided the furs which enabled them to purchase or barter for the basic material needs of the time.

## Along the Allegheny

The Tuscaroras, an Iroquoian speaking tribe from North Carolina, were accepted into the Iroquois Confederacy in 1722. The Tuscaroras had been engaged in a savage struggle with the British settlers in a vain attempt to stop them from taking their land and enslaving their children. They followed the roots to the Tree of Peace and settled in New York state.

In 1724 the Delaware Turtle and Turkey clans received permission from the Iroquois Confederacy (Six Nations) to migrate from the forks of the Susquehanna to the valleys of the Ohio River and Allegheny, building their first settlement at Kittanning.[16] This was the first significant settlement along the Allegheny since the Iroquois invasion.

The Allegheny River became of great interest to the French, the British, the Indians, the Virginians, and the Pennsylvanians, who by 1748 had begun to cross the Allegheny mountains and arrive here in great numbers. All of whom were seeking the fur trade or lands on which to settle. The French also had a vital interest in the area because the Ohio River System provided a line of communication between their southern territories and their northern territories. The river provided access to the Gulf of Mexico, access to passes through the Appalachian mountains, and it was rich in furs.

Captain Pierre Joseph Celeron de Blaineville carried out an expedition down the Allegheny and into the Ohio in June of 1749. The expedition departed Montreal on June 15th, 1749, and was comprised of approximately two hundred and thirty five men. There were fourteen officers and cadets, twenty French soldiers, and under the command of Chabert Joncaire (a trader), one hundred and eighty Canadians along with twenty Indians. They departed in twenty three large canoes, approximately thirty feet long, and ten smaller canoes carrying supplies. This arduous expedition was accomplished with many trials along the way. [17]

### Indian Nations in Western Pennsylvania
### 1725 AD

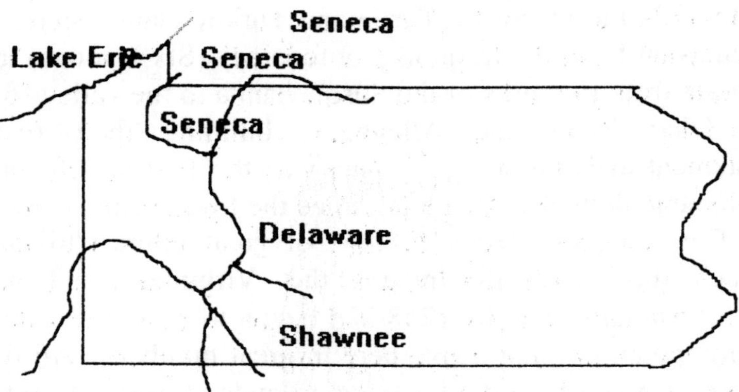


Celeron departed Montreal and paddled his way down the St. Lawrence River along the south shore of Lake Ontario arriving at the Niagara River. They portaged around the falls placing their canoes into Lake Erie at Buffaloe Creek, and proceeded along the south shore of Lake Erie coming to a marked point along the shore that indicated the portage trail to Lake Chautauqua. The soldiers then labored for seven incredible days through the dense forest, in the daily misery of rain, until arriving at Lake Chautauqua. The distance being approximately seven miles, averaging only a mile a day for progress. They launched their canoes into Lake Chautauqua and paddled their way to the southern tip of the lake, encountering shallow water and swamp. The party departed the lake by a small stream that led to the shallow Cassandra Creek and into the shallow Conawango Creek. This last part of the journey required the men to drag their canoes across rocks and through swamps damaging some of the canoes. It was no easy journey. They arrived at the Allegheny on June 29th, 1749, where present day Warren, Pa is located.[18]

The purpose of the expedition was to claim the Ohio River Valley for France. Celeron deposited a series of lead plates proclaiming the land to belong to his homeland. The first plate was placed on the south bank of the Allegheny opposite the mouth of Conewango creek in Warren, PA. The second plate was placed at a bottom where Snyder creek enters the

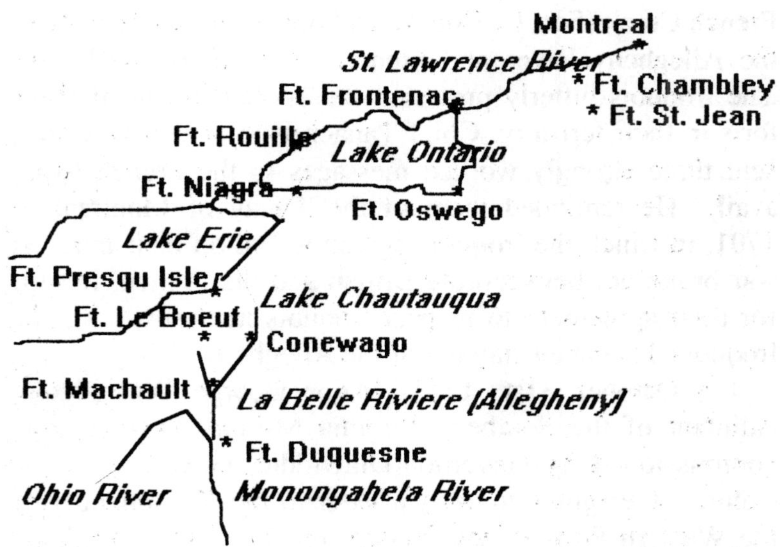


Allegheny, nine miles below French creek. The inscription on the plates stated that they were buried "as a monument

of renewal of possession which we have taken of said river, and all its tributaries, and of all the land on both sides, as far as to the sources of said rivers;" He stopped briefly at Attique (Kittanning) observing a village of approximately twenty cabins. He made reference to these Indians as being Loups, a French term meaning wolves. The Loups were most likely members of the Munsee clan of the Delaware Indians. The Delawares began settling on the Ohio around 1720 and by 1750 all of them were in Western Pennsylvania and Ohio. The third, fourth and fifth plates were buried at the mouths of Wheeling Creek, the Muskingum River, and the Great Kanawha.

In 1753 and 1754 the French built a series of Forts between Lake Erie and the Allegheny River, one on the shore of Lake Erie (Presque Isle), one at the headwaters of French Creek (Fort Le Boeuf), and one at the confluence of the Allegheny River and French Creek (Fort Machault). The Iroquois bitterly protested the encroachment of these forts in their territory. Chief Tanachrison, a Seneca Chief, sent three strongly worded messages to the French to no avail. He reminded them of the Treaty of Montreal in 1701, in which the Iroquois agreed to "sit on their mats" if war broke out between the British and the French, in turn for their agreement to respect Iroquois neutrality. To the Iroquois this meant stay out of the Allegheny Valley.

On October 31st, 1753, Major George Washington, Adjutant of the Southern Virginia Military District, was commissioned by Governor Dinwiddie, Governor of the Colony of Virginia, to carry a letter to the "Commander of the Western Forts of the French" on the Ohio (Allegheny River). Additionally, he was to gather military intelligence about the French Forces on the Ohio and adjacent areas. The purpose of Governor Dinwiddie's letter was to inquire

# Along the Allegheny

by "whose authority and instructions you have lately
marched from Canada with an armed force, and invaded

## Allegheny River 1749

Taken from Father Bonnecamp's Manuscript Map of Celeron's Expedition.

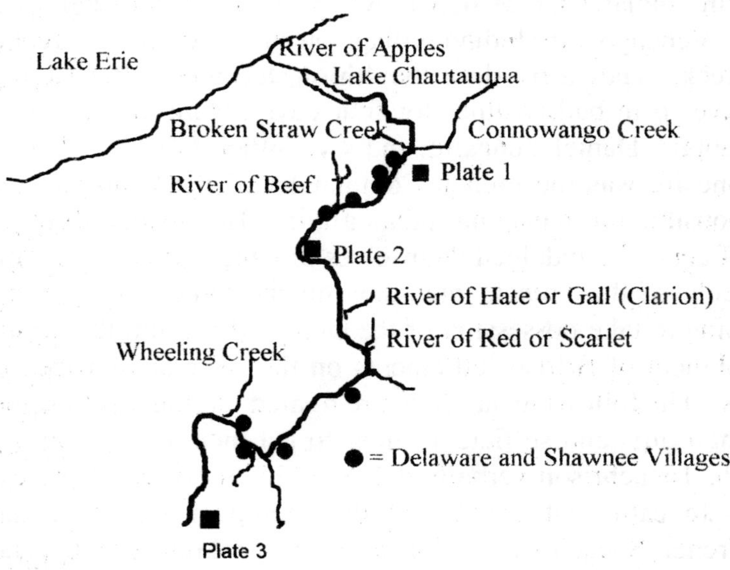


the King of Great Britain's territories."   The journey
required him to depart immediately.

He and Christopher Gist, an agent of the Ohio Company, arrived at John Frazier's at the mouth of Turtle Creek
on the Monongahela River on November 22nd. Frazier was
a trapper who was evicted from Venango by the French and
residing at the mouth of Turtle Creek on the Monongahela
River. They proceeded on to Forks of the Ohio where they
crossed the Allegheny River.  They traveled on to Log-

17

stown, west of the forks and along the Ohio River, were they met with the Sachems of the Six Nations (Iroquois League). There they solicited information on the where abouts of the French posts and support from the Indians for their mission.

On November 30th, Major Washington, Mr. Gist, Tanachrison, White Thunder, and Jeskakake (the last three being Indian Chiefs) departed by way of the Venango Trail to Venango, an Indian village at the mouth of French Creek. They arrived on the 4th of December after having traveled in bad weather for four days. Here, he met with Captain Daniel Joncaire and two other French officers. Joncaire was the French Commander of the Ohio and responsible for managing Indian affairs. He dined with these officers who indulged themselves in wine and began to talk freely of the French intentions on the Ohio. They were going to take possession of the Ohio and prevent the establishment of British settlements on the river or its tributaries. The following day Joncaire treated the Indians to some small gifts and sufficient liquor to get them drunk. On the 6th, Tanachrison verbally delivered his message of protest to Joncaire but unsuccessfully attempted to return the "French Speech Belt". Joncaire refused to accept it. The Speech Belt represented the Treaty of Montreal. On the 7th they departed for Fort Le Boeuf, travelling in terrible weather conditions through swamps and mires. The creek was high and fast and they were not able to cross, forcing them to travel on one side. Four days later they arrived at Fort Le Boeuf on the 11th of December.

On the 12th he met with Captain Jacques Legardeur de St. Pierre. The French officers held a council of war on the 13th to respond to Governor Dinwiddie's letter. On the 14th he received his response which simply stated that the

governor's message would be forwarded to the Marquis Duquesne, Governor of New France, and that the French
would remain at their posts.  The French then detained his
departure until the 16th by promising the Indians gifts of
guns and liquor.  The intent was to keep the Indians from
departing with Major Washington in order to win their loy-
alty from the British.  The six day journey back to Venango
was undertaken by canoe.  It was a very treacherous trip in
fast flowing, ice cold water with many portages over
shoals.  They arrived at Venango on the 22nd.  Major
Washington, Mr. Gist, and the remainder of his party,
excluding Tanachrison and White Thunder, who had been
injured, departed on the 23rd.  Mr. Gist and Major
Washington gave up their mounts as pack animals because
the other draft horses had become weak and feeble from
the arduous journey.  The horses got weaker, the weather
got colder, and the roads became worse with ice and snow.
After three days Major Washington decided to leave his
party and pursue a more direct route through the woods,
hoping that he could make better time.  He and Mr. Gist
left the trail near Murdering Town and made directly for
the Allegheny River.  Shortly after leaving the trail, Major
Washington was shot at by and Indian from 15 paces away,
but fortunately the Indian missed.  He and Mr. Gist were
able to capture the Indian and held him captive until 9 PM
then releasing him.  They then hurried on their way through
the night, hoping to get well ahead of the party of Indians
whom they suspected would be following them.  The two
of them continued travelling until dark the following
evening.  They arrived at the Allegheny River about two
miles from what was called Shanopin's Town, now Etna,
and there they built a raft to cross the river.  The raft got
caught in an ice jam and Washington was thrown into the

icy water. He managed to get back on the raft, however they were not able to free the raft from the ice causing them to abandon the raft for a nearby island where they spent the night in the freezing cold. Mr. Gist had his fingers and some toes frostbitten. In the morning the river had frozen over enabling them to cross and make their way to Frazier's home on the Monongahela river. He finally arrived at Williamsburg, Virginia on January 16th, 1754 presenting the letter to Governor Dinwiddie[19].

In the meantime, the Governor had already dispatched Captain William Trent (a trader) and a detachment of about thirty three militia to proceed to the Forks and construct a fort. The fort, Fort Prince George, was still under construction on April 17th, when it was captured without a fight by a superior French force. This force consisted of approximately five hundred men with eighteen pieces of cannon, which had came down river from Fort Le Boeuf in sixty Bateaux and three hundred canoes, and was under the command of Captain Claude Pierre Pecaudy de Contrecoeur. The men were allowed to leave with their tools and no harm was done to them.

The Indians, friendly to the British, made several requests for arms and ammunition to fight the French. The Quaker government of Pennsylvania ignored the problem of the Indians in the west who drastically needed the arms, ammunition, and other supplies promised them. The government withheld these supplies for two reasons: the French were now at Venango, and if they were given to the Indians they could be captured by the French. Additionally, since these lands had not been surveyed, Pennsylvania questioned its own authority west of the Alleghenies. Did this land belong to Pennsylvania or Virginia? By now, many of the Indians between Presque

# Along the Allegheny



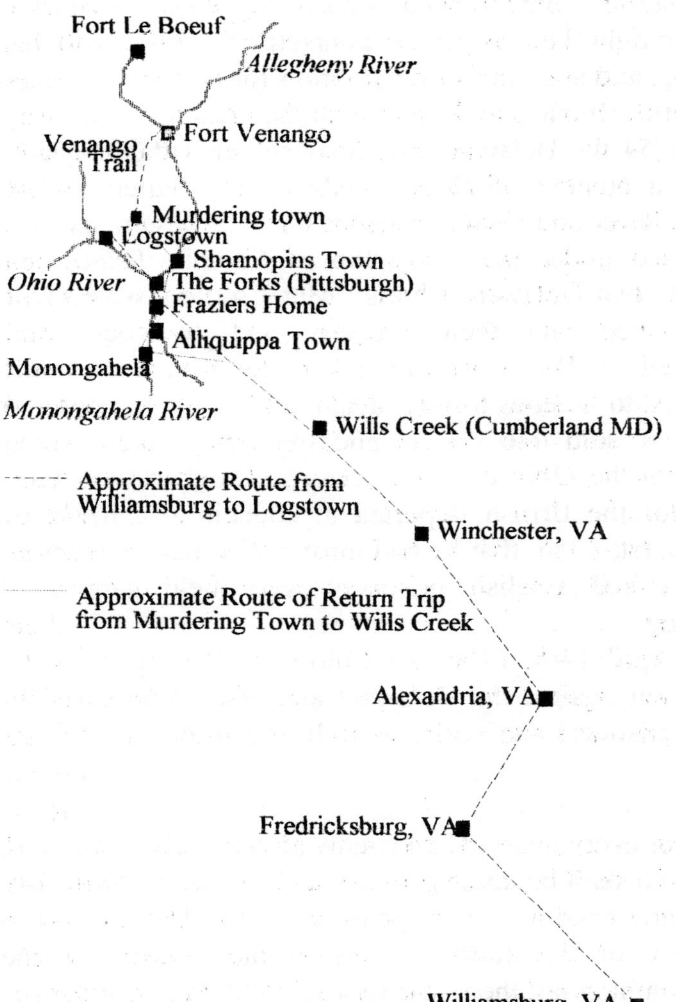


Isle and the Forks had allied themselves with the French. However, the Iroquois, Delaware, and Shawnee nations continued to remain neutral through the spring of 1754. In April of 1754, Tanachrison pleaded to the Governor of Virginia stating "Come as soon as possible, you will find us as ready to fight them as you are yourself"[20] This did not last for long, and soon out of desperation for necessities, many more of the Indians took sides with the French.

In 1754 the Delaware and Shawnee at Kittanning conducted a number of bloody raids on the settlers on the Juniata River and Conococheaque Creek. These raids were conducted under the leadership of Captain Jacobs and Shingas, two Delaware Chiefs. Many settlers were killed or captured and their property and livestock were destroyed. The prisoners taken to Kittanning were subjected to hideous torture, death, and cannibalization, or they were sold into slavery and frequently taken further west into the Ohio country. George Croghan, an Indian agent for the British, reported at council in Carlisle on January 1st, 1756, that he had information that as many as one hundred English prisoners were held captive at Kittaning.

On April 14th, 1756, the Colony of Pennsylvania declared war against the Delaware and offered bounties for Indian prisoners and scalps as well as returned white captives.

> For every male Indian enemy above twelve years old, who shall be taken prisoner and delivered at any fort, garrisoned by the troops in pay of this Province, or at any of the county towns to the keepers of the common jail there, the sum of 150 Spanish dollars or pieces of eight; for the scalp of every male enemy above the age of twelve years, produced to evidence of their being killed the sum of 130 pieces of eight;

for every female Indian prisoner and brought in as aforesaid, and for every male Indian prisoner under the age of twelve years, taken and brought in as aforesaid, 130 pieces of eight; for the scalp of every Indian woman, produced as evidence of their being killed, the sum of fifty pieces of eight, and for every English prisoner that has been killed and carried from this Province into captivity that shall be recovered and brought in at the City of Philadelphia, to the Governor of this Province, the sum of 130 pieces of eight, but nothing for their scalps; [21]

In retaliation for these raids, Colonel John Armstrong with three hundred and seven militia, attacked Kittanning on September 8th, 1756. According to Colonel Armstrong's report, September 14th, 1756 the following events occurred. The attack followed an arduous journey from Fort Shirley in Huntingdon County. Approximately six miles prior to reaching Kittanning their scouts spied a small party of three Indians sleeping along the trail. They left their horses and baggage at this point with a squad of twelve men to attack and kill this supposedly small party of the Indians in the morning. The main body of his battalion sized army left the trail and proceeded through the hilly terrain to the Allegheny River, arriving at a point approximately 1,650 feet below the village. Following this final thirty mile march the men spent the evening in silence with many of them sleeping. It was a warm, moonlit night and the Indians were settling down after an evening of dancing, many sleeping in a corn field. At daybreak, Colonel Armstrong deployed some of his men along the top of a nearby hill and then vigorously attacked the corn field while another party attacked the cabins. The fight ensued, many Indian women and children fled for the woods, while a fierce battle raged for the houses. The corn field and cabins were set on fire resulting in several Indians being killed while trying to escape the flames. Captain Jacobs was killed while trying to escape his burning cabin. The cabins then began to explode with a loud roar as the large quantities of gunpowder stored within ignited. The explosion from Captain Jacobs cabin blew the leg and thigh of an Indian and a small child to "such a height that they appeared as nothing, and fell into the adjacent Corn field". Shingas was not killed in this action but escaped and moved further into the Ohio country.

Following this action Colonel Armstrong began his return with the help of some captured horses to carry his wounded. He was sniped at from the woods by the Indians who had escaped the attack on the village. Fear dwelled in the hearts of the militia that they may be attacked by more Indians at any moment. To complicate matters, some of the men became apprehensive, fearing an ambush from the Indians on their return. Several of them under the command of a wounded Captain Mercer left the main body of troops, taking with them four of the freed captives.

Upon his arrival at the point where he had stored his baggage and tied his horses he found that the twelve men left to destroy the small group of Indians had been severely beaten. It turned out that the number of Indians spied along the trail had been grossly underestimated. There is reason to believe they had actually stumbled upon a raiding party which had been sent out from Kittanning the previous day. The number of Indians, although unknown, was greatly superior to his own force of twelve men. The skirmish began at daybreak and this small band of men were soundly defeated, some being killed or mortally wounded, while others deserted in the heat of battle.

In Colonel Armstrong's report he notes that thirty cabins were burned, thirty to forty Indians were killed or mortally wounded, and twelve scalps were taken. His losses included seventeen militia killed, thirteen wounded (including himself), and nineteen missing. He further states that he "retook" eleven English prisoners. Four of the freed prisoners left the returning body of militia with a Captain Mercer and twelve of his men, never returned. These men were believed killed or captured by the Indians.[22]

The French continued to control the Allegheny until General John Forbes and six thousand British regulars and militia (provincials) successfully drove the French from Fort Duquesne in 1758. However, the advance towards the Fort had a heavy price to pay due to the overly aggressive attempts of Major James Grant, an officer set on obtaining the glory of capturing Fort Duquesne with the forces under his command. On September 14th, 1758, Major Grant leading a very large reconnaissance unit of eight hundred men, Highlanders and Provincials, arrived at a hill once known as Grants Hill in Pittsburgh. Major Grant ordered Major Andrew Lewis and his four hundred Provincials to execute a bayonet attack on the sentries and Indians camped near the Fort. It was about two AM, when this action commenced. However the provincials got lost in the fog and the corn fields and fence lines surrounding the fort and returned to Grants Hill where Major Grant was waiting. This infuriated Major Grant who then sent a party of fifty men to attack some Indians which they had seen near a cabin. However, there were no Indians to be found at the cabin upon their arrival. The cabin was set on fire resulting in alerting the French to the presence of their British enemies in the area. At seven AM Major Grant sent a party of one hundred men to reconnoiter the fort. The provincials, under Major Lewis were sent back to the pack train to prepare for a possible ambush.

Major Grant was informed that the Indians had discovered his location, and as a matter of instilling confidence in his troops, played reveille to muster his men. The Commandant, Francois Marchand de Ligneris, sent several hundred French and Indians to immediately attack Grant's Highlanders at the center of Grant's forces, while others worked their way up along the banks of the Allegheny and Monongahela Rivers and attacked the flanks of the force. Major Lewis, hearing the din of the battle, returned with his provincials and engaged the enemy as best as he could with fighting being scattered through the area.

Major Grant retreated under intense fire and panic spread to many with thoughts of the Braddock disaster in mind. The retreat or route continued until the remainder of his force reached an area near Arsenal Park where their baggage had been stored under the protection of Captain Bullet and fifty Virginians. The fight continued until Captain Bullet suggested they deceive the enemy into thinking they were surrendering. They raised a white flag, holding their rifles above their heads, and moved toward the Indians who had now emerged and gathered in the open. Major Grant's Forces then opened fire on the Indians and routed them with a bayonet charge. Captain Bullet and his men escaped. Major Grant with a few soldiers fought to the end at the edge of the Allegheny River, where he was captured. Many of the captured Highlanders were taken to Fort Duquesne and tortured to death by the Indians. The Major was spared.[23]

## Along the Allegheny

Following Major Grant's defeat and hearing of the approaching army of General Forbes, the French burned and abandoned Fort Duquesne.  On November 25th, 1758 General Forbes and the main body of his army marched triumphantly into the remnants of Fort Duquesne.  They built a small fort, Fort Mercer, and then Fort Pitt, named after William Pitt, England's great statesman.

No sooner had the French abandoned Fort Duquesne and the British took it over as Fort Pitt, did the rumblings of the second contest begin.  Christian Frederick Post was a German Moravian who came to Pennsylvania in 1742.  He attempted to convert the Indians in western Pennsylvania and elsewhere to Christianity.  In 1758, under orders of the Governor of Pennsylvania, he proceeded west to visit the Shawnee, the Mingo, and the Delaware.  His mission was to persuade these Indians to remain loyal to the English during the French and Indian War.  Frederick Post received two warnings from the Indians in the valley.  The first warning came on November 28th, 1758 from Chief Beaver of the Delaware's, who said "I would tell you in a most soft and loving friendly manner to go back over the mountain and stay there; if you will do that, I will use it as an argument, to argue with the other nations."  He received a second warning from Kittiuskund, a Delaware counselor, who said "All the nations had jointly agreed to defend their hunting place at 'Alleghenny,' and suffer nobody to settle there . . . if the English would draw back over the mountain, they would get all the other nations in there interest; but if they staid and settled there, all the nations would be against them; and he was afraid it would be a great war, and never come to peace again." [24]  These warnings of war would later be borne out by an Indian Revolt called  Pontiac's War.

## Along the Allegheny

After the defeat of the French at Niagra on July 24th, 1759, the British gained control of the Allegheny Valley. The French abandoned their posts at Fort Machault, Fort Le Boeuf, and Presque Isle at what is now Erie. Prior to abandoning Fort Machault the French had been busily preparing for an attack on Fort Pitt. Approximately one thousand Frenchman and an equal amount of Indians had gathered at Fort Machault in July of 1759. They busied themselves building bateauxs (large canoes) and piroques (dugouts) for the descent down river to Fort Pitt. They were almost ready for their attack when they, as well as the other garrisons of the other two forts, received orders to abandon their plans and bring all their forces to Niagra where they were desperately needed. The Fort and everything which they could not take with them was burned to keep it from the hands of the British. The Indians were generously given the stores and foodstuffs that were not burned and were promised that the French would return the following year.

"The History of Venango County" shows an early drawing of Fort Machault which looks like the drawing below.

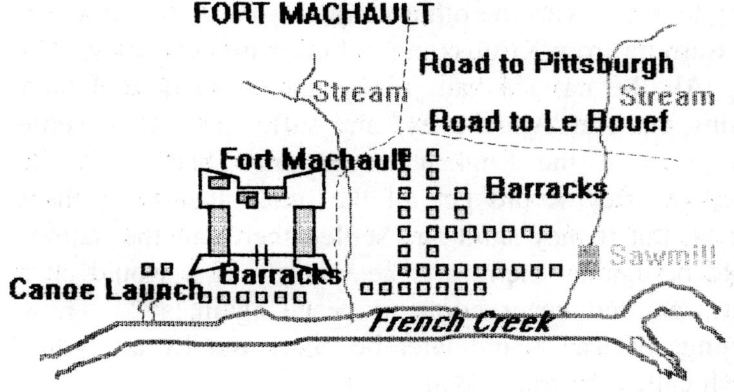

# Along the Allegheny

At first the Indians rejoiced because they believed they would get their hunting grounds back along the Allegheny, however this failed to be the case. All things considered, the Allegheny Valley was considered Indian territory prior to the French invasion, as perceived by the Iroquois and understood by them in the Treaty of Montreal. Now, the British had driven out the French and their Indian allies, and to the consternation of the Iroquois, Delaware and other Indian tribes, had entrenched themselves in the valley in lieu of the French.

The British built a new fort during the summer of 1760, about six hundred and sixty feet above the previous Fort Machault. The new fort was called Fort Venango, but did not last long. They also reestablished Fort Le Boeuf and Fort Presque Isle now under British command. In January of 1763 the French and British signed a formal treaty of Peace with the British now possessing the Allegheny Valley to the frustration of the Indians. With continued French encouragement, a second contest was beginning to brew in the Allegheny Valley and elsewhere. Pontiac, a Chief of the Ottawas, was determined to drive the English back across the Alleghenies.

The British did not treat the Indians very well following the expulsion of the French from the valley. They no longer had any competition from the French in buying furs and took advantage of the Indians. The British traders also took advantage of the Indians thirst for rum and many an Indian woke from a drunken slumber to find himself cheated out of his furs. Robert Rogers, an Indian agent at the time, wrote the following passage in "Ponteach".

A thousand Opportunities present

To take Advantage of their Ignorance;

But the great Engine I employ is rum, . . .

That cooling Draught well suits their Throats.

Their Fur and Peltry come in quick Return;

My Scales are honest, but as well contriv'd,

That one small Slip will turn Three Pounds to One;

Which they, poor silly Souls! Ignorant of Weights

and Rules of Balancing do not perceive.[25]

White settlers continued to cross the Alleghenies frequently posing as trappers or hunters, but quietly seeking out lands for farming. Bouquet wrote the following: "these lands have been run over by a number of Vagabonds, who under pretense of hunting, were making Settlements in several parts of them of which the Indians have made grievous and repeated complaints."[26] All efforts by the Colonial and English governments to stop the entry of white settlers on Indian lands failed. Soon war came to the Allegheny Valley.

The "Hounds of Hell," as Ensign John Christie called them, came violently to Presque Isle. At dawn on June 15th, 1763, Fort Presque Isle came under attack from two hundred Indians who had departed Detroit expressly to destroy this fort and to capture or kill its inhabitants. This fort was a vital communication link between the settlements along the lake and Fort Pitt through the

# Along the Allegheny

Allegheny River and French Creek connection. The fort was well built and believed to be impregnable with a large blockhouse from which the defenders could fire at the enemy. It was located on the south side of Lake Erie with the block house in the corner of the fort. This block house was supposed to be impenetrable offering a commanding position from which two walls of the fort could easily be defended. However, it was too close to the lake and a small stream, the banks of which would provide cover for the attacking Indians.

Inside the fort were twenty seven men under the command of Ensign John Christie. They were well prepared, excluding a shortage of ammunition, for the onslaught which was to follow. Ensign Christie was not interested in starting a battle with the Indians when they appeared before the fort. As a result they were allowed to get too close, and when he finally fired at them they took cover in the nearby creek. They began to fire intensely at the fort and to shoot flaming arrows in an attempt to set the fort on fire. Soon they managed to set up three breastworks of logs closer to the fort, enabling them to fire more accurately into the fort's loopholes and throw fire balls of pitch into the fort.

The inhabitants continually had to put out fires, eventually running out of water. There was a well in the center of the fort. It was impossible to reach because it meant exposing one's self to the hostile fire. The ingenuous inhabitants tunneled to the well and were able to continue to put out fires started by the Indians. The battle continued through the night with no rest for the defenders. There was a period of relief in the morning, but the battle resumed again in the afternoon. By now the defenders were exhausted. The siege dragged on until midnight, when the Indians spoke to them through a former English soldier, who had been previously captured and had defected to the Indian's cause.  The soldier told them that if they continued to resist that the fort would be set on fire from "above and below at once."  If they surrendered they would not be harmed.  Ensign Christie requested and was granted until morning to make his decision.  The inhabitants at first decided to continue to resist.  In the morning Ensign Christie sent two soldiers out to mediate with the Indians and observe their capabilities to burn the fort.  Returning to the fort, Ensign Christie then met half way with two Indian chiefs and surrendered the fort on the promise that the inhabitants would be unharmed and allowed to go to Fort Le Boeuf, which would have been the nearest post.  However, upon their surrender the inhabitants were made captives and taken to Detroit.  One individual escaped, Benjamin Gray, who darted into the woods and made his way to Fort Pitt were he told them of the disaster at Fort Presque Isle.  He also told them that he passed both Fort Le Boeuf and Fort Venango, both of which had been burned to the Ground.  The Allegheny Valley now was embroiled in Pontiac's War.[27]

The situation at Fort Le Boeuf was not much better.  There was a small detachment of fourteen men stationed at the tiny post of Fort Le Boeuf under the command of Ensign George Price of the Royal Americans.  The post consisted of a blockhouse which was poorly constructed.  There was a shortage of ammunition and poor quality powder.  In the morning of June 18th a small party of Indians were admitted into the blockhouse were they asked for "powder and ball" to fight their enemies the Cherokee.  They were refused and spent the night sleeping in front of the blockhouse where they were joined by thirty more Indians.  The Indians begged for a kettle to cook their food, but this could not be done without opening the door to the fort which Ensign Price refused to do. The Indians tore the blocks from a foundation of a nearby storehouse and entered it and from there they were able to fire at the blockhouse eventually setting it on fire. The battle raged until the defenders were no longer able to tolerate the smoke and flames. Finally Ensign Price and his squad escaped during the night out a small rear window of the blockhouse.

They attempted to make their way in the dark through a pine swamp to Fort Venango. Some of them got separated from Ensign Price and the others. The group continued to wander in the dark woods all night. In the morning they found themselves no further than two miles from Fort Le Boeuf. They continued the trek to Fort Venango having only three biscuits apiece for the journey. Upon arriving at Venango, they found that the fort had been burned to the ground. The inhabitants were found dead in the ashes and ruins of the fort. Ensign Price and the remaining members of his detachment eventually found their way to Fort Pitt. It took three excruciating days of walking without food, other than the biscuits they had when they left and whatever edible plants and berries the woods could provide. Two of the stragglers never returned and were presumed to have died in the wilderness.[28]

The worst tragedy took place at Fort Venango. The only information about the destruction of Fort Venango and the killing of its defenders is that told by an Indian who claimed to have participated in the attack. Accordingly, a group of Senecas entered the fort under the guise of friendship and killed the compliment of soldiers found inside. They forced the commander, Lieutenant Francis Gordon, to write a letter explaining their grievances. Soon after he was slowly tortured to death. The Indians burned the fort before leaving.[29]

Fort Venango had "heavy earth works, with a ditch surrounding it, and a magazine and soldiers quarters in the interior. It also had a covered way leading down to the stream of water on the southern side. The main work was eighty eight feet square. Outside of this was a ditch twenty four feet wide, and outside of this an embankment. The out-look covered the mouth of French Creek." The site was located about 220 yards above the former Fort Machault.[30]

War between the Indians and the British continued with ferocity. Both Fort Ligonier and Fort Pitt at the southern extremities of the Allegheny valley were attacked, as well as numerous settler's forts and homesteads. Fear caused many of the settlers on the Pennsylvania frontier to retreat over the Allegheny Mountains to safety. At one point in time, July 25th 1763, there were one thousand three hundred and eighty four refugees in Shippensburg.[31] All of whom had abandoned home and hearth in the Allegheny Valley in fear of Pontiac's warriors and their relentless raiding and scalping of any white settlers west of the Allegheny Mountains.

Sipes, in The Indian Wars of Pennsylvania, relates this story from "Henry Bouquet." Andrew Byerly and his family lived near Bushy Run on Brush Creek. Mr. Byerly had left his home to bury the remains of settlers who had been killed by Indians some distance away, leaving his wife, newborn child and three other children alone for the night. A friendly Indian came to their home at night and warned them that they would all be killed if they did not make their escape before morning. Mrs. Byerly left a note on the door of her cabin informing her husband of her actions and left during the night. She gathered her milk cows, and with a three day old infant in her arms, a toddler strapped behind her on the horse, and a three year old walking or being carried by his older brother, they began a thirty mile journey to Fort Ligonier. The cattle slowed their progress and had to be abandoned in the forest for fear that the Indians would catch the small party as they traveled through the woods to Ligonier. Mr. Byerly caught up to his family and all made it safely to the fort, which came under attack the following morning after their arrival.[32]

Fort Ligonier, in the south eastern region of the Allegheny Valley came under attack about the same time as Fort Le Boeuf and Venango. Fort Ligonier was defended by a Lieutenant Archibald Blane with a small garrison of Royal Americans and terrified refugee settlers who had scurried to the fort seeking protection. This was a key post because of the arms and ammunition stored there. If these weapons and ammunition would have be taken by the Indians it would have greatly enhanced their ability to wage war both east and west of the Allegheny Mountains. The Fort came under attack by Indians around the end of May (the Thursday preceding June 4th 1763). Lieutenant Blane had the neighboring houses burned to keep the Indians from seeking refuge and fortification in them. On the Sunday prior to the 17th a man wandered out of the fort and was killed. The Indians attacked the fort again on the 28th but were driven off after an intense two hour battle. On July 1st a group of twenty expert marksmen (woodsmen) arrived at Fort Ligonier from Fort Bedford and shortly thereafter approximately thirty Highlanders accompanied by more woodsmen arrived at the Fort from Carlisle. These men traveled at night to avoid detection and finally entered Fort Ligonier under fire from the surrounding Indians.  At Fort Pitt the story was a different matter.

Captain Simeon Ecuyer, a Swiss mercenary then in command at Fort Pitt, prepared his fort by hardening (making bullet proof) the barracks for the protection of women and children, repairing the ramparts, and erecting palisades.  Communication beyond the fort was not possible during that July, due to the numerous raiding parties active in the area.

## FORT VENANGO

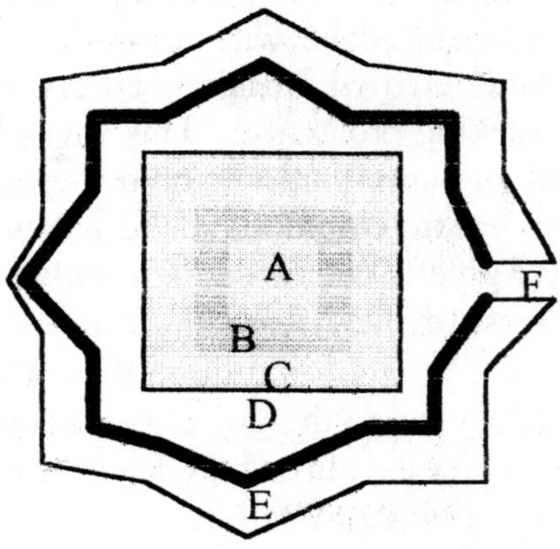


A  Bldg 60 x 50 feet with cellar for magazine
B  Grounds between ditch and Bldg were 88 x 88 F´
C  Ditch 7 feet deep and 24 feet wide
D  Bastions and picket walkway
E  Embankment 7 feet high inside and 8 feet outside
F  Entrance

To compound matters, several of the inhabitants in the fort were suffering from Smallpox and a Smallpox infirmary had been built under the drawbridge.  During the course of the battle a small group of Delaware Indians approached the fort carrying a British flag and requested to speak to

Captain Ecuyer. They were admitted to the fort, among whom were Chiefs Shingas and Turtle Heart in an attempt to peacefully take over the fort. In this they failed, and not only did they fail but Captain Ecuyer gave them two blankets and a soiled handkerchief from the Smallpox Infirmary. A tactic that had been approved by General Amhurst, Commander of the British forces in America, and

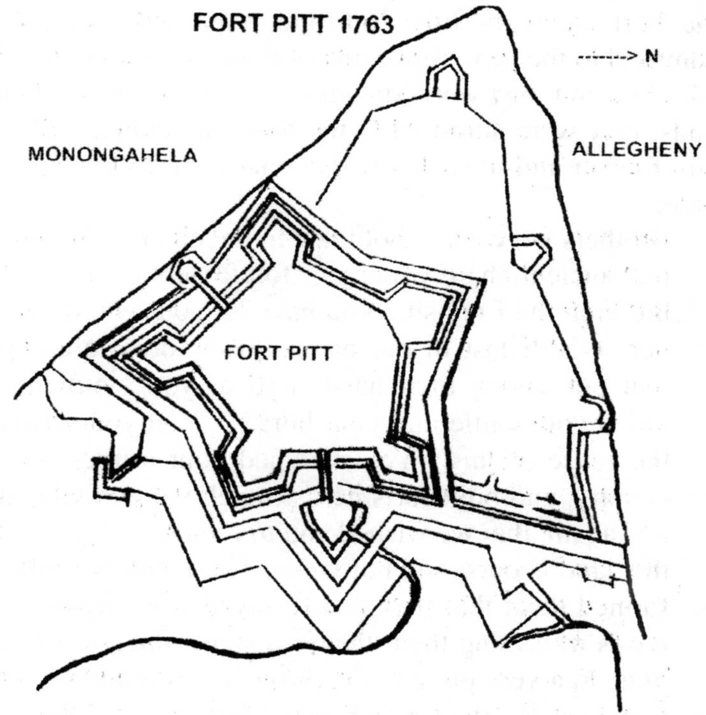


The above drawing is based on upon an an excellent drawing of Fort Pitt by Charles Stoltz.[33]

Colonel Bouquet. Captain William Trent noted in his journal on June 24th: "Out of our regard to them we gave them two blankets and a handkerchief out of the Smallpox

Hospital.    I hope it will have the desired effect."[34]
Although it cannot be ascertained that this action alone
resulted in the following Smallpox epidemic that occurred
among the Ohio tribes, it certainly reflects their intentions,
which were fueled by animosity between the British and
Indians at the time.    It can be said that neither Colonel
Bouquet nor General Amhurst had any love for the Indians.

Shingas, Turtles Heart, and several others approached
the Fort again on July 26th and requested that they be
admitted to the fort.  Since one of them was carrying a British Flag, and they were known to be friendly to the inhabitants, they were admitted to the fort.  In council with Captain Ecuyer and his officers they made the following state-
ment.

> Brothers we wish to hold fast to the chain of friendship,
> that ancient chain which our forefathers held with their
> brethren the English.  You have let your end down, but
> ours is still fast in our hands.  Why do you complain
> that our young men have fired at your soldiers, and
> killed your cattle and your horses.  You yourselves are
> the cause of this.  You marched your armies into our
> country, and built forts here, though we told you, again
> and again, that we wished you to remove.  My Brothers
> this land is ours, and not yours. These chiefs further in-
> formed them that they had received word from the Ot-
> tawas informing them that in a short time we intend to
> pass, in a very great body, through your country, on our
> way to strike the English at the forks of the Ohio.  The
> Delaware chiefs then warned if you leave this place
> immediately and go home to your wives and children,
> no harm will come of it; but if you stay, you must
> blame yourselves alone for what may happen.
> Therefore we desire you to remove.[35]

Captain Ecuyer's response to this entreaty was very direct. He informed them of the strength of his fort and warned them of dire consequence that would befall them if they attacked the fort.

> I have warriors, provisions, and ammunition to defend it three years against all the Indians in the woods; and we shall never abandon it as long as a white man lives in America. I despise the Ottawas, and am very much surprised at our brothers the Delaware, for proposing us to leave this place and go home. This is our home. You have attacked us without reason or provocation: you have murdered and plundered our warriors and traders: you have taken our horses and cattle; and at the same time tell us your hearts are good towards your brethren the English. How can I have faith in you? Therefore now, Brothers, I will advise you to go home to your towns and take care of your wives and children. Moreover, I tell you that any of you appear again about this fort, I will throw bombshells, which will burst and blow you to atoms, and fire cannon among you, loaded with a whole bag full of bullets. Therefore take care, for I don't want to hurt you.[36]

On the 27th of July, the Indians proceeded with a night attack on the fort. They surrounded the fort, seeking cover along the banks of the rivers and digging, similar to what we would now call, "foxholes" to shelter them from the forts defensive fire. The morning brought an increase in combat which lasted all day until evening. This battle continued for several days with the Indians receiving the worst of it.

## Along the Allegheny

The siege continued until August 1st, at which time they disengaged in preparation to attack Colonel Henry Bouquet and his small army struggling to reach Fort Pitt. On August 5th and 6th, the Indians engaged Colonel Bouquet and his force of Highlanders, Light Infantry, and Royal Americans at Bushy Run, about twenty three miles from Fort Pitt. They were out maneuvered and soundly defeated by his smaller, disciplined, combat experienced, and well trained little army, causing their retreat from the Allegheny Valley. This was a major defeat for the Indians.

Although the Indians had moved many of their villages from the valley, they still continued to raid the farms of settlers in the border areas near the Allegheny Mountains throughout the summer of 1764. So fierce were these attacks on the Pennsylvania frontier, that the English Governor of Pennsylvania proclaimed:

> premiums and bounties for the prisoners and scalps of the enemy Indians that shall be taken or killed within the bounds of this province, . . . for every male Indian enemy above ten years old who shall be taken prisoner . . . the sum of one hundred and fifty Spanish dollars, or pieces of eight. For every female Indian enemy, taken prisoner . . ., and for every male Indian enemy of ten years old or under, taken prisoner . . . the sum of one hundred and thirty pieces of eight. For every scalp of every male Indian enemy above the age of ten years, produced as evidence of their being killed, the sum of one hundred and thirty-four pieces of eight. And for the scalp of every female Indian above the age of ten years, produced as evidence of their being killed, the sum of fifty pieces of eight."[37]

The result of this proclamation brought out the worst in some whites who indiscriminately killed Indians, friend or foe, to collect the bounty for their scalps.

The hostilities resulted in further campaigns by Bouquet and Bradstreet into the Ohio Country. On October 15th, 1764, Colonel Bouquet met with the Indians (Delawares and a band Senecas) along the Muskingum River and under the overwhelming presence of one thousand five hundred armed soldiers with bayonets glistening in the sun, the Indians sued for piece. They were given twelve days to surrender all their prisoners and to provide them with clothing, food, and a horse to transport them back to Fort Pitt. Over two hundred captives were returned at that time. About one hundred more were returned from Shawnee villages following this event. Many of whom had been fully accepted into the tribes that had taken them captive and had no desire to be separated from their Indian families. It should be noted that the Shawnee did little to comply with the peace that Colonel Bouquet made with them. The Shawnee turned over only a few prisoners keeping approximately one hundred and fifty of them until the following Spring. They were contemptuous of the treaty to the point that an Indian killed Colonel Bouquet's footman the following day, and sporadic hostilities continued between whites and Indians leading to Lord Dunmore's War in 1774.[38]

In 1768, at the Treaty of Fort Stanwix the British completed an agreement with the Iroquois Confederacy that allowed the Indians to maintain a large portion of the northern and western area of Pennsylvania, which included the Allegheny River. This boundary begins near Fort Sullivan following the North Branch of the Susquehanna River south to the Sheshequin Path, which travels in an irregular south westerly direction, to where it intersects the West Branch of the Susquehanna River near Williamsport. It continues west along the West Branch of the Susquehanna to Clearfield, then directly to Kittanning where it follows the Allegheny south to its confluence at Pittsburgh with the Ohio, and following the Ohio westward to the Mississippi River.[39]

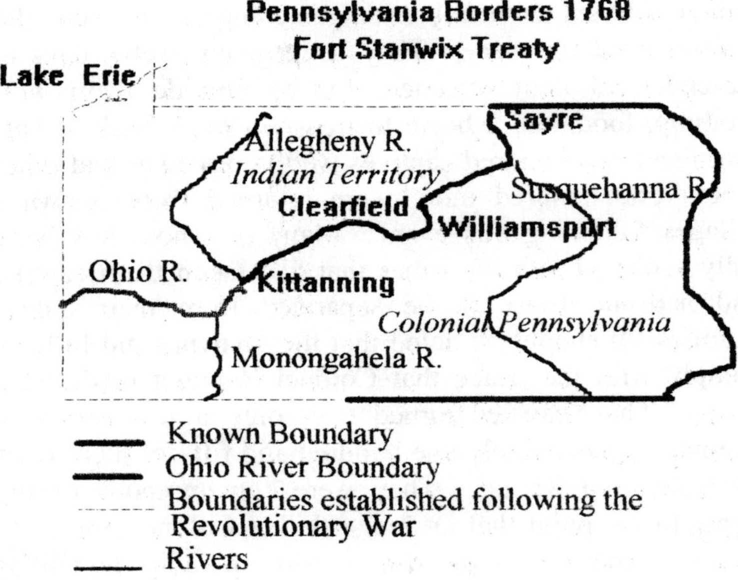



The Allegheny River continued to be an area of contention and struggle between the Pennsylvanians and the Indians during the Revolutionary War. The Americans ratified the Treaty of Fort Stanwix at the Treaty of Pittsburgh in 1775. White settlers and trappers continued to flow into Indian land in violation of the treaty and the British encouraged the Indians to "Take up the Tomahawk" against the settlers. Panic soon spread and fear of attacks by both white settlers and Indians, based on rumors and isolated incidents, spread throughout the area. This panic fueled the fires of animosity and racism increasing the hostilities of both the white settlers and the Indians. The Mohawk, the Mingo, some of the Seneca and other tribes took sides with their old ally the British.

The fear of the barbarities and cruelties that the Indians dispatched during warfare is often reported, however very little has been said about the barbarism and cruelties of the whites in venting their animosity on the Indians. This is probably due to the Indians not being able to keep a written record of these acts. However Heckewelder stated the following about the Indian and white cruelties.

> The Indians are cruel to their enemies! In some cases they are, but perhaps not more so than the white men have sometimes shewn themselves. There have been instance of white men flaying or taking of the skin of Indians who had fallen into their hands, then tanning those skins, or cutting them in pieces, making them into razor-straps, and exposing those for sale, as was done at or near Pittsburgh sometime during the revolutionary war. [40]

In 1779 Colonel Daniel Brodhead planned an expedition up the Allegheny into the heart of Seneca country to "prevent future hostilities on the part of the Seneca and to 'revenge the past, to carry the war into their country and strike a decisive blow at their towns'." A second reason was that General Sullivan was carrying out a campaign against the Iroquois in New York State and this was to be a diversionary action. Colonel Brodhead evacuated Forts Randolph, Laurens, and Hand and erected Forts Armstrong and Crawford along the Allegheny.[41]  He had difficulty obtaining support from the militia as well as limited supplies to support the mission.

Instead of four months of supplies he was only able to obtain one month's provisions for the campaign.[42]  There were two reasons for the shortage of militia and supplies. First, there were relentless attacks by the Indians on the settlements in southwestern Pennsylvania causing the militia to stay home and protect their families and property. These attacks resulted in the death or captivity of many settlers and the destruction of their farms and livestock.  The most significant of which occurred at Fort Hand on the Conemaugh, on April 26th and 27th.  Over one hundred Indians sieged the fort for two days.  The siege was not lifted until the arrival of Colonel Lochry of Westmoreland and the county militia.[43]

The second reason for his shortage of supplies was that the Deputy Quartermaster was having difficulty getting drivers to haul the goods from Carlisle to Pittsburgh.  It is hard to believe that in the early days of our country something as critical as this could be hampered by bureaucracy. However, most of the drivers had militia commitments to their county and the county magistrates fined them if they failed to report for militia duty.[44]

In June of 1779, three rangers, who had been on a reconnaissance mission to Venango in Seneca country were chased from Seneca country by a number of warriors in canoes.  This chase continued down river until they had passed Kittanning.  The men narrowly escaped with their lives.  Following this incident, Colonel Brodhead ordered Captain Samuel Brady and a party of twenty rangers and a young Delaware Chief by the name of Nannowland (also known as George Wilson) to Seneca country.  Meanwhile, the Seneca's were venturing south to raid the settlements of southwestern Pennsylvania. They killed a soldier between Fort Crawford and Fort Hand along the Kiskiminetas River. They proceeded to Sewickley where they killed a woman and her four children and took two children captive.[45]

Captain Brady and his party encountered an Indian raiding party at what is now called Brady's Bend. He surrounded them and attacked them at the break of day. Several Indians were killed or mortally wounded, the rest escaping into the forest. Captain Brady retook two captives, six horses, scalps and plunder. He also took the rifles, tomahawks, matchcoats, moccasins, and anything else belonging to the dead Indians.

As a result of these raids Colonel Brodhead ordered the erection of a fort at Kittanning (Fort Armstrong). He believed that this fort would stop the incursion of Indian raids into Bedford and Westmoreland counties. However, the raids continued.[46]

Colonel Brodhead received permission for a campaign against the Senecas on the upper Allegheny. He prepared sixty boats, some of which were canoes, skiffs, and dugouts. Colonel Brodhead began the expedition up the Allegheny on August 11, 1779 with about six hundred men, mostly regulars and only two small companies of rangers with a few Delaware Indians. The main body, along with a small number of cattle, proceeded on shore along the river while his supplies were transported up the river by boat. When supplies and men had arrived at the Big Mahoning, his force departed the Allegheny and traveled by way of an old Indian trail through Clarion county eventually arriving at Tionesta Creek. A few miles north of Brady's Bend, Brady and about thirty rangers observed a party of thirty warriors heading south under the lead of Delaware Chief

Bald Eagle.  After sending back a runner to inform Colonel Brodhead, he and his rangers took cover in the forest, allowing the party of warriors to pass. Colonel Brodhead set up an ambush for the warriors, but it was prematurely started when one of his men dropped his rifle causing it to discharge, accidentally killing himself in the process.  As the Indians retreated up the trail they were fired upon by Brady's Rangers, killing Chief Bald Eagle and four others and wounding several more. Continuing north to Tionesta, they found an abandoned village called Quoshquoshink. They crossed the Allegheny River and continued north to Brokenstraw Creek and an Indian village called Buckalloons.

Captain Brady and his Rangers surprised a Seneca party about three miles south of Brokenstraw Creek where they spied four canoes with warriors coming down the Allegheny River. Each canoe carried approximately twelve warriors.  The Rangers immediately took cover and established a plan to lure the Indians to shore.  The warriors were led by a Seneca Chief Dehguswaygahent and a Munsee Chief Dayoosta.  One of Brady's men, named Nicholson, went to the shore and attracted the warriors attention.  They immediately headed for shore and disembarked with weapons in hand. Nicholson had now disappeared into the forest, but they spotted a ranger by the name of Jonathan Zane peering from behind a tree and immediately fired at him. He received a light wound in the thigh.  Brady's Rangers then commenced firing from their places of hiding with deadly effect.  Fifteen Indians were killed and fourteen were wounded and fled into the forest or the river.  A canoe full of about twelve Indians swiftly paddled out of sight and escaped.  Captain Brady's men suffered only a few casualties with no one being killed.

They took the rifles and ammunition, as well as the Indians provisions. Colonel Brodhead left a party of forty men to care for a wounded man along with the remainder of his provisions and continued to advance up the Allegheny River, destroying abandoned villages along the way and ending his campaign near present day Warren.

The Colonel met little opposition because most of the warriors were away fighting General Sullivan. Upon his arrival at the upper reaches of the Allegheny he found the Indians living in houses (log cabins), some of which were large enough for three or four families. He destroyed one deserted Seneca town and seven Munsee (Delaware) towns. At the town of Yoroonwago, Colonel Brodhead's soldiers "destroyed one hundred and thirty houses and five hundred acres of growing corn and took plunder, including furs, to the amount of thirty thousand dollars."[47] On his return he burned the towns of Connewango (Warren), Buckaloon, and Mahusquechikoken (north of Franklin). He followed the Venango trail from French Creek back to Fort Pitt.

The campaign was a difficult one, since he had traveled over three hundred miles through very rugged terrain. Many of his soldiers had worn out their shoes due to travelling over the rocky terrain, and their clothing had been torn to shreds from the brush. The sight of his barefoot and half naked men prompted Colonel Brodhead to send an immediate request to President Reed for shoes and clothing for the soldiers who completed the campaign. His letter stated "I have neither shoes, shirts, blankets, hats, stockings, nor leggins to relieve their necessities."[48] This excruciating ordeal provided only temporary relief for the settlers on the Pennsylvania frontier as well as points east of the Allegheny mountains.

## Along the Allegheny

The struggle for the Allegheny Valley did not end here. Many of the Iroquois had been "dragging their feet" during the war until now. This changed dramatically. As a result of the attacks into the Iroquois Country by General Sullivan and Colonel Brodhead, the Iroquois with the support of their British allies intensified there attacks into Pennsylvania. The Indians continued to raid travelling unimpugned up and down the Allegheny River striking settlements deep into its into its lower tributaries. The year of 1780 became known as the "Year of Sorrows." [49] It was so bad that Pennsylvania placed a one thousand dollar bounty on Indian scalps. [50]

The British also offered a bounty on American scalps. Allan Eckert, in his book "The Dark and Bloody River" presents a letter from the British Secretary of Indian Affairs in Albany New York to the British Governor of Montreal, that accompanied several bundles of scalps. These scalps were taken by Seneca warriors and other Indians from the upper reaches of the Allegheny river and elsewhere. The letter, dated January 3rd 1782, indicates that the British paid for one thousand and six American scalps. The letter further indicates that the scalps were taken from men, women, children, and infants. Only forty three of these scalps were taken from "Congress" soldiers, while the vast majority were taken from settlers in western Pennsylvania and what is now West Virginia. [51]

On July 13th, 1782, a work party was harvesting a crop at O'Conners farm on the out skirts of Hannastown when one of the workers saw a small group of Indians moving toward them from a neighboring field. Having warned the others everyone ran to town, gathered up friends and family and went to the nearby fort. Four men on foot and one on horseback departed the fort to reconnoiter the location and number of Indians. The man on horse back was seen by the Indians causing him to take flight and warn the others. Upon warning one family, he took a second rider on his mount and continued in desperation to Hannastown. The men on foot returned to the fort. The riders went into town to warn any possible remaining townsmen, and after a brief altercation with an Indian whom he killed, they made their escape to the fort.

There were only about twenty five men in the fort and only about fifteen rifles, making for a slim defense of the fort. A group of approximately three hundred Indians and whites (possibly Loyalists or Canadians) arrived to attack the fort. As the Indians laid siege to the fort a small child ran into an open space and unknowingly exposed him or herself to the Indian line of fire. A young women rescued the child but was mortally wounded in the effort. This was the only known casualty in the attack on the fort. The town was looted and burned.

During the battle at the fort, a large body of Indians disengaged themselves from the siege and attacked nearby Millerstown. A young couple had been married that day and a reception was being held at a "Mansion" in Millerstown. The remainder of the people were busy going about their daily activities. Those in the fields managed to make their escape into the woods, but the wedding party suffered at the hands of the Indians. Mr. and Mrs. Jack Brownlee, guests at the reception and the entire wedding party were made captives. The Indians departed with their captives and shortly thereafter recognized Jack Brownlee as a well known Indian fighter. He was carrying his child on his back when an Indian murdered him with a tomahawk, then killed his child and an accompanying female captive who began to scream. Mrs. Brownlee watched in horror and silence in great fear for her own life.  The remaining prisoners were taken to Canada and turned over to the British.  They were released following the war in 1783.

While the raid at Millerstown was taking place, the fort at Hannastown continued to resist the siege by the Indians. That night thirty armed men from nearby had assembled and marched to the fort, and after some cautious reconnoitering of the Indians whereabouts, they proceeded directly to the fort under cover of darkness.  During the night, the settlers had both men and horses  traverse back and forth, several times, over the bridge that led to the fort in order to deceive the Indians into thinking that reinforcements had arrived.   They also played military music on a drum and fife to impress them that regular soldiers were among them. This deception worked and the Indians left in the night.

When the British were defeated, the Americans no longer felt the previous treaties between the British and the Indians were valid and the Indians found themselves abandoned by their former British allies.  Following the Revolutionary War,  a second treaty was signed at Fort Stanwix (1784) and Fort McIntosh (1785), giving the United States (the 13 Fires as they were referred to by the Indians)  all that territory which had been  previously recognized in the 1768 treaty as belonging to the Indians. The entire Allegheny Valley within Pennsylvania was now in the hands of the Americans.  This area now includes the counties of Crawford, Butler, Venango, Forest, Warren, McKean, Clarion, Jefferson, Elk, Cameron, Potter, parts of Beaver, Allegheny, Armstrong, Erie, Indiana, Clearfield, Clinton, Tioga, and Bradford.   However, many of the Indians did not accept this treaty and they continued to resist Pennsylvania's settlement of the area.[52]

# Along the Allegheny

Waterman, Watkins, and Co. relate the following story in the "History of Butler County."[53]  On March 23rd, 1792, a small band of Indians comprised of Senecas, Munsees, and others attacked the John and Massy Harbison cabin near Reed's Station, a blockhouse near the mouth of the Kiskiminetas River.  The Indians killed one man, two small children, and wounded a third man, Mr. Wolf, who made it to the blockhouse approximately two hundred yards away. Mr. Harbison was away on a "spying" mission as a ranger. Mrs. Harbison, flogged and beaten, was taken prisoner along with her "young child" and was claimed by one of the Indians for his wife.  Holding her infant in her arms, she observed the murder and scalping of her two boys.  The five year old was killed at the cabin for resisting the Indians.  The three year old was killed for complaining and not being able to keep up.  He had been injured when a horse fell while descending the east bank of the Allegheny. They crossed the Allegheny River proceeding west to Buffaloe Creek, which they also crossed.  Pursuing their westerly course they crossed the Little Buffaloe Creek and finally the Connoqunessing Creek, stopping near Butler. They cleared a place in the brush to sleep for the night. Without something to drink, and being unable to eat due to facial bruises she had received from her captors, she spent the night with her arms tied behind her back and dreaming about her escape.  She was moved on the second night, but remained in the area.  She escaped the following morning before dawn.  After the first day of travel she realized she was going in the wrong direction.  She spent the first night in the wilderness and changed direction the following morning toward the Allegheny River.  The second evening, as she prepared to make a bed out of leaves, she put her infant down and the baby began to cry.  Hearing footsteps, she hid herself and infant among the branches of a large fallen tree until she was sure her pursuer had left.  She had to stuff clothing into her baby's mouth in order to keep her infant from crying.  The Indian left after standing and listening in the area for two hours.  She then left her hiding place and traveled about a mile were she settled down for the night.

On the fifth day of this excruciating experience in the forest, she unknowingly crossed Pine Creek and following the path along its bank came across moccasin tracks and an abandoned cooking fire.  She left the trail, being concerned that the tracks and fire may have been made by Indians.  After traveling about three miles she came upon a cow path and followed it to an abandoned cabin.  Exhausted and ready to lay down and die from her ordeal, she heard a cow bell which spurned her on.  With thoughts of her infant's survival foremost in her mind,  she followed the sound and came to the bank of the Allegheny River opposite a blockhouse at Six Mile Island.  She was rescued by James Clossier, one of her former neighbors.  Mrs. Harbison was so beaten, emaciated, and suffering from scratches and imbedded thorns from her ordeal, that he did not recognize her.  She was cared for by the people in the blockhouse, where one hundred and fifty thorns had been removed from her feet.  John and Massy Harbison were reunited in Pittsburgh.

As late as 1794, history records the trials of Captain Andrew Sharp, Mr. Connor, Mr. Taylor, Mr. McCoy (unmarried) and their families involved in a deadly encounter with hostile Indians.  This group of twenty individuals was in the process of emigrating from the Plum Creek area in present Armstrong County to Kentucky where Captain Sharp had obtained some land by trading his property at Plum Creek.  They began their journey in the Spring of

# Along the Allegheny

1794 at Black Lick Creek, where they had built a flatboat and loaded it with their personal belongings and some live-stock. After proceeding down Black Lick Creek, they entered the Conemaugh River and continued on eventually entering the Kiskiminetas River. The party had rafted as far as the mouth of Two Mile Run and put the huge raft ashore. Captain Sharp went back up stream to retrieve a canoe that had been detached from the flatboat prior to entering the falls upstream. When he returned just prior to sunset they were informed by a man that there were Indians in the area. The women and children then got into the boat and the horses were tied ashore. They had planned on making it to a nearby home of an individual by the name of David Hall, when they were fired upon by seven Indians. Captain Sharp was grazed in the right eyebrow. Mr. Taylor jumped on a horse and ran off into the woods. Captain Sharp was wounded two more times, while cutting the boat loose. He had now been wounded at the eyebrow, on his left side, and on his right side. Somehow, they managed to get the boat away from the river bank. Captain Sharp then shot one of the Indians. However, unfortunately for the families in the boat, the boat got caught in a whirlpool and continued turning in a circle exposing the people on board to more gunfire from the Indians. They managed to get the boat moving downstream and into the Allegheny River. The Indians followed it down the Allegheny for about twelve miles while continuing their attack on the boat. During the terrible journey Mr. McCoy and the oldest son of Mr. Connor were killed. Mr. Connor was severely wounded. Miraculously, none of the women or children were killed. Mrs. Sharp took control of the boat through the night. The next morning they found themselves about nine miles from Pittsburgh, and seeing some men on shore hailed them for help. The men assisted them in getting to Pittsburgh and sent someone ahead in a canoe to prepare for their arrival. Captain Sharp died from his wounds July 8th, 1794, and he was buried with full Military Rites, having been a veteran of the Revolutionary War.[54]

From the beginning of the French and Indian War in 1754 to the Treaty of Greenville in 1795, the Allegheny Valley was the scene of a continuous, violent, and bloody contest. A prolonged contest that pitted the French against the British, the Colonials against them both, and the Indians divided and eventually fighting everyone including themselves. A contest caused by the continuous westward movement of the restless, poor European immigrants, armies in conquest of new lands, land hungry speculators, and people in pursuit of the fur trade. While all along the Indians fought for possession of their "Alleghenee."

**Fort Le Boeuf about 1796**

## Along the Allegheny

Chief Cornplanter (known by the Seneca's as "Kaintwaton" meaning "one who plants") also known as John Abeel was a principle war chief of the Seneca's who resided in the upper Allegheny region. He played a powerful role in bringing about a settlement of the land problems and Indian relations following the Revolutionary War. His diplomacy in these matters resulted in the Pennsylvania General Assembly granting him and his heirs forever a 1,500 acre tract of land along the upper Allegheny which was commonly known as the Cornplanter Tract. The Kinzua Dam was built in 1964 on this tract of land, resulting in the inhabiting Seneca's being moved into the adjoining reservation in New York. [55]

Following the defeat of the Indian Coalition by General Anthony Wayne at Fallen Timber and the Treaty at Greenville in 1795, the Indian resistance in the Allegheny River Valley subsided. Early settlements along the river and its tributaries were:

| | |
|---|---|
| Allegany NY - 1820 | Olean NY - 1804 |
| Warren - 1795 | Tidioute - 1800's |
| Tionesta - 1816 | Oil City - 1803 |
| Clarion - 1801 | Kittanning - 1800 |
| Parker - 1800's | Pittsburgh - 1758 (Fort Pitt) |
| Port Allegheny - 1816 | Jamison Flats - 1797 |
| Ford City - 1807 | Franklin - 1754 (FT.Machault) |

Populations in the following Pennsylvania Counties along the Allegheny formed in 1800 were:

| | |
|---|---|
| Warren 230 | Venango 1,130 |
| Butler 3,916 | Allegheny 15,087 |
| Armstrong 2,399 | Lycoming 5,414 |
| Westmoreland 22,726 | |

# Along the Allegheny

## Chief Cornplanter, 1796, by F. Bartoli[56]

Collection of New York Historical Society #6338

# Along the Allegheny

## Forts and Indian Villages
## 1700 - 1800 A.D.

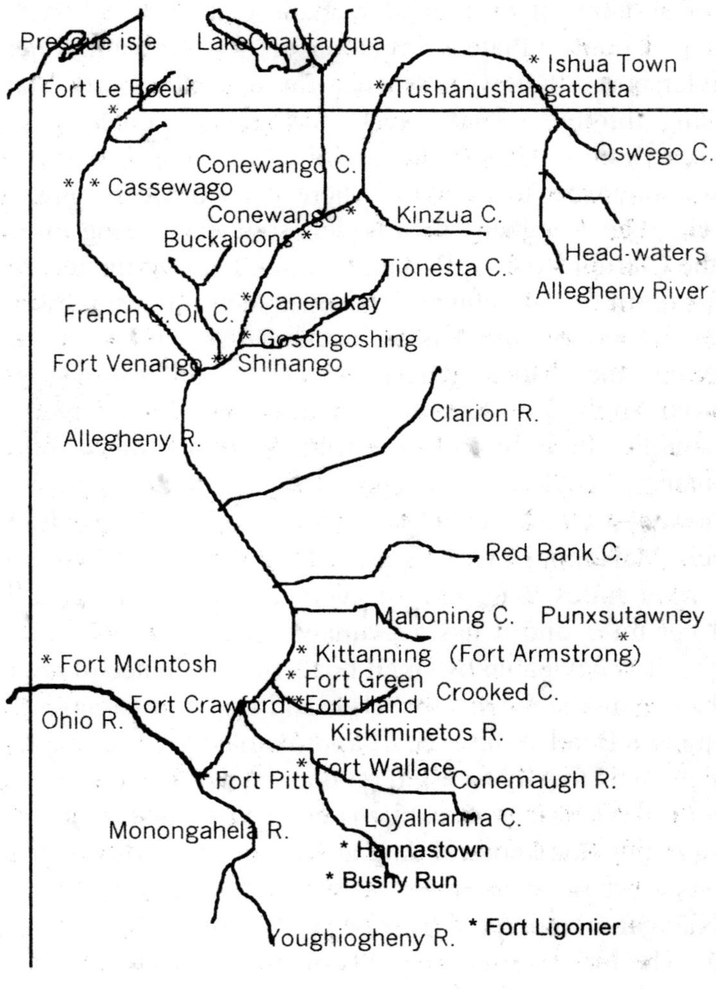

## Early Navigation

The Allegheny River is the main headwater to the Ohio River system.  It rises at an altitude of 2,250 feet in the Potter County Plateau region of Pennsylvania near Coudersport.  It flows northwest through New York State passing through Olean and Salamanca entering the Kinzua Dam, Allegheny Reservoir.  From the dam it then flows southwest to Franklin where it is joined by French Creek.  The Allegheny then travels southeast, being joined by the Clarion River at Parker, to a point approximately ten miles north of Kittanning.  The river then turns southwest, being joined by the Kiskiminetas River, and continues meeting the Monongahela River at an altitude of approximately 730 feet and creating the Ohio River at Pittsburgh.  In addition to the tributaries mentioned, other tributaries include Oswego Creek, Kinzua Creek, Conewango Creek, Tionesta Creek, Oil Creek, Red Bank Creek, MaHoning Creek, and Crooked Creek.  The river is 325 river miles long, has an average slope of about 4.55 feet per mile, and it has a drainage area of 11,778 square miles.  It is navigable by small boats for a distance of about 200 river miles above Pittsburgh and by commercial craft to Brady's Bend, a distance of approximately 72 miles. The Allegheny is mostly forested on both banks which makes it popular for boating.  It contains eight locks and dams and has a major flood control dam at Kinzua.  In addition there are six other flood control dams within the watershed.[57]

Navigation along the river began with the Indians in the area.  The Indians used dug-outs or vessels made of elm or other bark.  Canoe birch was not available in the Allegheny Valley.  There is a place at the headwaters of the Allegheny near Port Allegheny at the mouth of Portage Creek which was once called Canoe Place.  If you follow Portage Creek upstream to top of the Allegheny divide and cross the divide you will find another stream, also called Portage Creek, which flows to the Driftwood branch of the Sinnemahoning, near Emporium, and becomes part of the Susquehanna Watershed.  Early travelers, Indians and trappers, were known to use these portages to gain access to the Allegheny and Susquehanna River Valleys.

"Coureurs de bois"[58] or runners of the forest were known to paddle their canoes at a rate of forty eight strokes per minute, which could move a canoe at great speed. Trappers and traders measured the time from place to place by the number of pipes of tobacco they smoked.

Olean NY. (also known as Olean Point or Hamilton) began as a debarkation point for travelers anxious to move west into the newly acquired Ohio Territory.  Travelers ventured to this community during the winter when the roads were hardened by the frost and built make shift shanties to protect them until the Spring thaw.  When the snow began to melt and the Allegheny was free of ice, these poor, weary travelers embarked by flat boats down the Allegheny heading for south western Pennsylvania, Virginia, or lands along the Ohio.  In the summer the river was plagued with low water and exposed shoals.  In the Spring and Fall the river was frequently disturbed by high velocity flood waters. Travel was difficult in any season.[59]

Hamilton was a small village, which included one large hotel, Hicks Hotel.  This hotel was known to accommodate up to two hundred people at a time, however the accommodations were probably strained. Food shortages were a major problem.  "Upon such occasions flour sometimes sold at Olean Point at twenty five dollars per barrel, and pork at fifty dollars, and other necessary articles in proportion." Less fortunate people were often forced to beg from others and ask their assistance to continue their journey's.[60]

Travel and commerce developed quickly along the river. Flatboats, arks, keelboats, and eventually steamboats provided the means of travel. William Darby, 1818, stated in his "Emigrant's Guide to Western and Southwestern Territories"

> Hamilton, at the headwaters of the Allegheny River, is a small village, but from its situation has become a thoroughfare for families from the eastern states to the countries lying on the Ohio and Mississippi Rivers. Large Arks, twelve by sixty feet, roofed over, are sometimes built at Hamilton, on which families embark, with their wagons and horses. The distance from Hamilton to Pittsburgh, through the turns of the river, is 260 miles (254) and the only road by land is about 170, yet the direct distance is much short of that. The Allegheny is a steady stream and is navigable by arks and boats in the spring and fall and by occasional freshets in the summer.[61]

In 1818 an early traveler at Olean made these remarks describing arks.

> The ark was built of stout planks, with the lower seams caulked, forming a perfectly flat basin in the water. It was about 30 feet wide, 60 feet long, with Gunwales of some 18 inches. Upon this was a raised structure of posts and boards, about eight feet high, divided into rooms for cooking and sleeping, leaving a few feet of space in front to row and steer. The whole was covered

by a flat roof which formed a promenade, and near the front of this deck were two long sweeps, a species of gigantic oars which were occasionally resorted to, in order to keep the unwieldy vessel from running against islands or dangerous shores.[62]

**Ark**

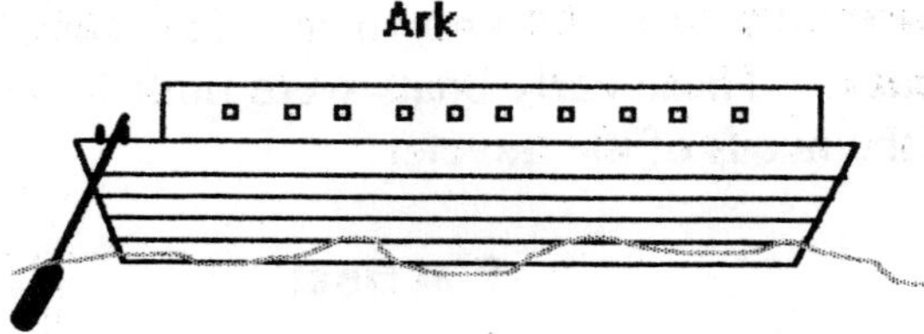

The Allegheny was later the birth place for several large ocean going vessels. In 1797 the Americans were having problems with Spain and France when sailing down the Mississippi River. The Mississippi River was occupied on both sides by those two countries. The American government became so concerned about the situation that they directed the building of two war galleys at Pittsburgh. These war ships built along the Allegheny River were named the President Adams and the Senator Ross, and they were launched on May 25th, 1798, and March 26th, 1799. Fortunately the conflict was avoided. Other vessels built at Pittsburgh (Alleghenytown) included a one hundred and seventy ton brig, called Dean. This ship was launched January 16th, 1803, and was known to continue its journey from the mouth of the Mississippi River to Liverpool, England.

The Pennsylvanians and New Yorkers began the use of flatboats, arks, keelboats, barges and steamboats. Flatboats were first put into use by the early settlers of the Allegheny River Valley. These settlers needed a larger conveyance to haul there families and household goods down the river. Flat boats (flat bottomed boats) began as not much more than rafts with or without shanty on top to keep the occupants dry. They had a rudder on the rear to help steer them and could be poled if necessary. These boats were usually torn apart at there destination and the lumber used for other purposes, causing them to be known as "The Boats that never came back." These early boats were built in various sizes to meet the needs of the traveler.

**Flat Boat**

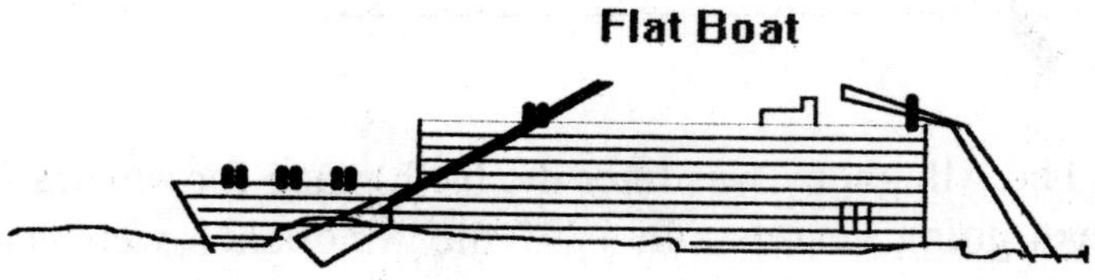

Flat boating freight and raw materials became a large endeavor and the size of flatboats increased to carry more materials from the upper Allegheny to points below such as Pittsburgh and beyond. In 1830, the Pittsburgh Gazette printed the following.

We are informed by good authority that between Waterford and Bemus on French Creek, a distance of twenty two miles, from ninety to one hundred flat bottomed boats are started or about to start for Pittsburgh. These boats are built principally by individual farmers and are freighted with hay, oats, potatoes, and various other kinds of produce; also bark, shingles, cherry and walnut lumber. The average freight of these boats is 27 tons, and an average value of the boat and cargo at Pittsburgh is $300. From Bemus Mills to the mouth of French Creek the number of boats of the above description is equal, if not greater, exclusive of rafts, which make a very considerable item, so that the trade of French Creek this season, may be safely estimated at $100,000.[63]

River traffic not only went down river but also up through French Creek to Lake Erie, where it continued to the Erie Canal and on to New York. This included large quantities of milk cheese and butter from the Allegheny Valley. Keelboats were used for both upstream and downstream transport and came into use about 1790. These boats were also widely used as a conveyance over the many miles of canals built in Allegheny Valley. They received their name from the long heavy piece of timber found in the center of the frame. They were pointed at both ends, up to seventy feet long, ten feet wide, carried up to twenty tons, and could be rowed or poled. The Keelboat was sloped downward towards the middle of the craft which helped keep the load centered. The drawing below does not reflect its concave symmetry.

**Keel Boat**

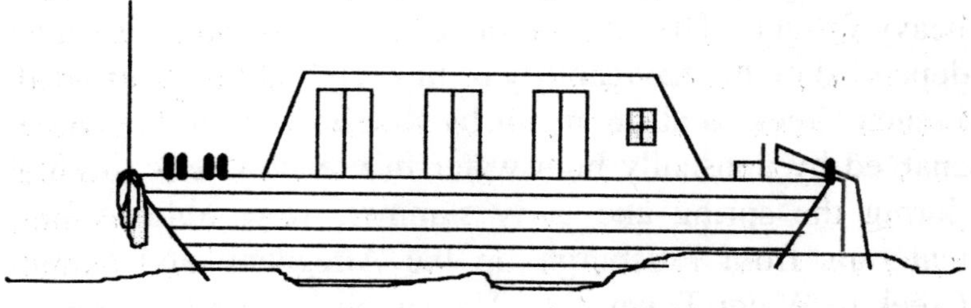

During the war of 1812 the Allegheny River played a significant role in the Battle of Lake Erie. Commodore Perry was directed to build a fleet of ships at Presque Isle to defeat the British fleet at Lake Erie. He was faced with a very difficult task as the only raw materials at hand were timber. All other materials would have to be located and brought to him from elsewhere. There were three developing communities that could provide him with what he needed. They were Cleveland, Buffalo, and Pittsburgh, all of them approximately of equal distance from Presque Isle. There were no railroads and what roads did exist were nothing more than muddy trails. The trails where widened paths cleared of brush, trees and stumps. These roads could not withstand the weight of heavy conestoga wagons, nor could they withstand the large and powerful teams of six horses which tore up the ground as they strained at their harness along the uneven terrain. Lake Erie was controlled by the British fleet, who by this time had captured most of the small number of American vessels on the lake, and whose presence negated any attempts by the remaining few vessels to sail the lake and deliver the needed materials to the Americans at Presque Isle. The only glimmer of hope was the Allegheny River and French Creek connection. Although the distance between Waterford and Pittsburgh by land is significantly shorter than it is by following the meandering Allegheny, the river could easily carry the heavy freight. The success or failure of building this fleet depended on the navigability of this river and high water in French Creek to allow travel by Keelboat. The keelboats, enabled by unusually high water in French Creek in 1813 during the spring and early summer, were able to haul materials from Pittsburgh up the Allegheny and French Creek to Water Town, Pa. The supplies were then hauled by horse and wagon to Presque Isle. Had it not been for the Allegheny River and French Creek, the fleet would not have been built at Presque Isle. The Battle of Lake Erie was the turning point in the war of 1812 resulting in American control of the Great Lakes.[64]

Following the war, the volume of traffic continued to grow and included lumber from Meadville and Warren and salt from western New York. Commerce dropped off somewhat with the opening of the Erie Canal. The Pittsburgh newspaper "The Mercury" reported on November 12, 1822, that:

> There is now lying at the mouth of Wayne Street in this city a shalloped shaped keelboat 35 feet long, with several families on board, who embarked on this boat at the mouth of Wood Creek, head of Oneida Lake, state of New York. The course pursued to reach Pittsburgh was by passing down Oneida Lake, and through Oswego River into Lake Ontario: thence up the Niagara to within five miles of the falls. The vessel was then carried around the falls on wheels and was again placed on wheels and carried seven miles along a good road to Chautauqua Lake and creek into Connenwango Creek, entered the Allegheny River at Warren, and arrived safely at Pittsburgh."[65]

The rivers on the western waters were frequently low with many shoals and sandbars protuding during the summer. An expert on steam boating in the early years, George Fitch, said that: (a riverboat) must be so built that when the river is low and the sandbars come out for air, the first mate can tap a keg of beer and run the boat four miles on the suds." Vessels designed for sea travel had difficulty travelling on the rivers.

In the 1820's steamboats began traveling up the Allegheny river. The steamboat Albion traveled from

**Along the Allegheny**

Pittsburgh to a few miles north of Kittanning  The steamer was under the command of Captain Parcell and is believed to be the first steamer to travel up the Allegheny River. This event proved it possible for travel further up the Allegheny, and opened up the prospect for future trade and navigation into the northern regions of Pennsylvania and western New York.[66]

The first steamboat to travel from Pittsburgh to Franklin was the William C. Duncan, a steamer of one hundred and ten tons.  The steamer, under the command of Captain Benjamin Crooks, departed Pittsburgh on February 22nd, 1828, and after stopping at Kittanning, Lawrenceburg and other places, arrived at Franklin on the 24th, at 5:00PM. The total distance was one hundred and forty miles.[67]

The Albion and the William C. Duncan were side wheel steamers.  In order to get further up the shallow waters of the Allegheny a new steamer needed to be built.  A man by the name of Blanchard had designed a steam engine and steamboat for use on the Connecticut River.  This twin wheel steamer had its wheels on the stern of the craft, and the design was found suitable for traveling the upper reaches of the Allegheny.  He found that the river had a depth of twelve inches or more between Kittanning and Franklin. Some stream improvement would be required, such as the removal of some large stones.  A boat was constructed sixteen feet wide and ninety feet long and named the "Allegheny."[68]

On April 15th, 1830, the "Allegheny" ascended the river of her namesake and after stopping at Freeport and Franklin along the way, arrived at Warren on April 19th.  This was a major event in Warren.  The local people foresaw a great future in navigation, particularly because the water was low due to a drought, but still deep enough to allow upstream travel by the little steamer.

The "Allegheny" departed Warren on the 19th on its final leg of the journey to Olean.  The small steamer struggled through the swift current and rapids, finally arriving at Olean Point on the 21st of May, 1830.  The steamboat now found itself two hundred and fifty four miles above Pittsburgh, at an altitude of approximately one thousand and four feet above sea level.  This too was greeted with great exuberance.

### Stern Wheel Steam Boat

Another river boat that made it to Olean was the "New Castle".  This boat was 100 ft. x 16.5 ft. x 3.5 ft. and weighed 40 tons.  Captain Josh Leach piloted this boat to Olean in 1837.  The New Castle was also the only steamboat to travel up the Kiskiminetas to Leechburg, the only river boat known to achieve this feat.  Other river boats that traveled the upper Allegheny were the  Major Andrian, also known as the Tidioute, which traveled from Pittsburgh to Meadville.  River boats that traveled from Pittsburgh to Warren and Brokenstraw were the Oneota,

## Along the Allegheny

Prairie Bird, Pulaski, Warren, and Wave No 2.[69] By 1835, three hundred and four out of six hundred and eighty four Steamships on the rivers were built in Pittsburgh. Pittsburgh had become the center for Steam Engine Manufacturing.

## The Allegheny River System

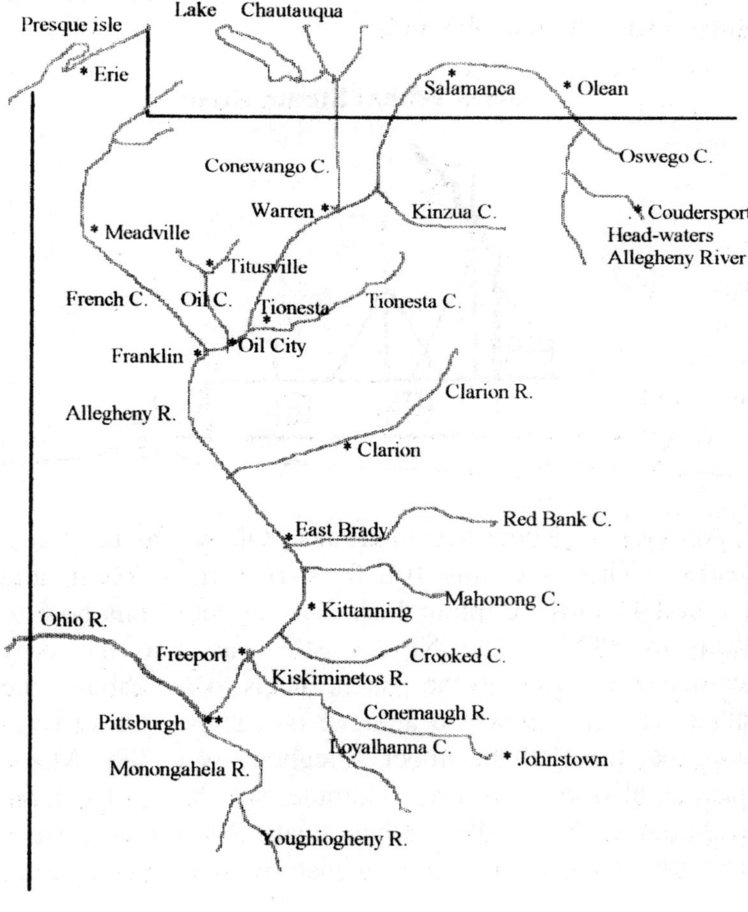

In addition to river traffic there also was a extensive system of canals that brought much business between the communities. The Pennsylvania Mainline Canal crossed the Allegheny River by via duct at Freeport and connected with the Western Division that went south west to Allegheny Borough on the North side of the Allegheny River. A terminal was built at this juncture. The terminal had a series of four locks that allowed the canal boats to be lowered into the Allegheny River. This terminal proved to be valuable when the aqueduct to be discussed was not working.[70]

The people of Pittsburgh were adamant that a the canal continue on through Pittsburgh and join the Monongahela River. A second aqueduct crossing the Allegheny River was built from Allegheny Borough to the intersection of Grant and Liberty in Pittsburgh, the longest aqueduct built on the Main Line Canal. This aqueduct was one thousand one hundred and forty feet long, sixteen and one half feet wide at the top, fourteen feet wide at the bottom, and was eight and one half feet deep. It was made out of a double layer of planks two and one half inches thick and had both a pedestrian walkway on one side and a tow path for horses or mules on the other side. In 1845 this aqueduct was replaced by one designed by John A. Roebling, the same individual who designed the Brooklyn Bridge. This new aqueduct was the first cable suspension bridge to be used in the United States.[71]

The next major project in connecting the Mainline Canal was a tunnel through Grant Hill. This too was an extraordinary feat. The canal included an eight hundred and ten foot long tunnel under Grants Hill and four additional locks to lower the canal boats to the Monongahela River. This was referred to as the Pittsburgh Canal Extension.[72]

Construction of the Western Division Canal was began in 1827. The canal was extended from Freeport to Kittanning a distance of fourteen miles, and was known as the Kittanning Feeder. The canal measured forty feet wide at the top of the water line and twenty eight feet wide at the bottom, and it was a minimum of four feet deep. The Western Division had sixteen aqueducts and one hundred and fifty two road bridges among an assortment of other construction devices. The canal saw its first fully loaded canal boat arrive in Pittsburgh from Johnstown in 1831 with seven thousand three hundred and ninety seven pounds of cargo.[73]

## Pittsburgh Aqueduct crossing the Allegheny

Front View

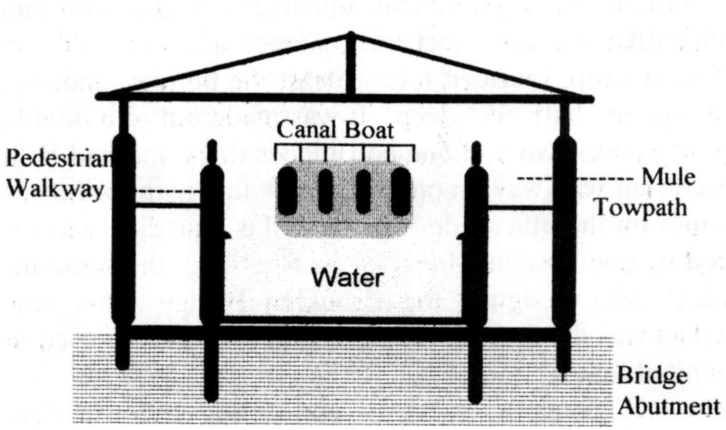


The Pennsylvania Main Line Canal which ran from Philadelphia to Pittsburgh was enhanced by the Beaver and

# Along the Allegheny

Erie Division. The Great Lakes region received most of its imports from Pittsburgh. At that time the main route of transportation was up the Allegheny River to Franklin, from there up French Creek to Waterford, from Waterford to Erie by wagon, and finally by sailing ship to various destinations on the Great Lakes. The citizens of Erie, who at the time were dependent on Pittsburgh for much of their trade and commerce, lobbied the Pennsylvania Legislature heavily for access to the Pennsylvania Canal. On February 25th, 1826, the state authorized what became known as the French Creek Connection. This canal connected Franklin, Meadville, and Conneaut Lake to the Allegheny River.[74]

In 1831 a thirty one mile section of canal system to connect Erie with Pittsburgh via the Ohio River was started. This section began at Beaver on the Ohio and went as far as Pulaski by way of the Beaver River and Shenango River. These rivers were improved to handle canal traffic.[75]

In February of 1836, the Shenango Division was started. This comprised the digging of a canal from Pulaski to Conneaut Lake a distance of sixty one miles. The final leg of the Pittsburgh to Erie canal system was called the Conneaut Division. It began in 1838 and required forty five miles of digging. The canal project was turned over to the Erie Canal company who completed the final project in 1844 and the canal was opened for traffic.[76]

The total cost of the project was approximately $4,500,000. The entire canal system from Beaver to Erie included one hundred and thirty six miles of canal, one hundred and thirty seven locks, thirteen dams, thirty basins, and two hundred and twenty one crossing road bridges. The completed canal linked the northwestern communities to the Pennsylvania Mainline Canal and the Allegheny River System.[77]

# Along the Allegheny

## Allegheny River System and Canals

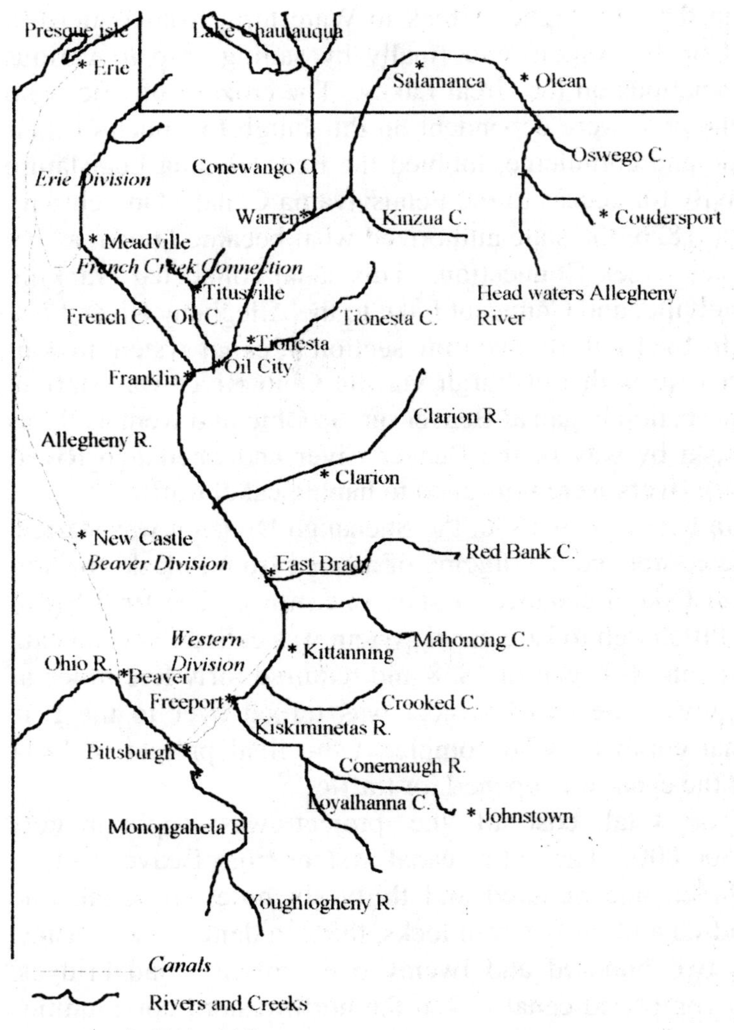

# Summary

From the earliest days of civilization along the Allegheny River, through the building of the canals in western Pennsylvania, the Allegheny River Valley has proven itself to be a valuable resource. It was near the heart of the Monongahela civilization and later became the center of the struggle among the Iroquois and other tribes for it furs. When the French invaded the valley in 1754 the Iroquois protested and joined with the British to have them expelled from their Valley. When the British established their forts in the Valley, the Indians once again rebelled and fought to stop the spread of Colonial civilization into their "Alleghenny." Their attempts at driving the Colonials back across the Allegheny Mountains were futile and the onslaught of western civilization continued its ever encroaching march westward. The Revolutionary War brought with it hopes for the Indians of regaining their precious valley, but only in their loss did they finally submit to the treaties turning it over to the Americans, and this was done with continued resistance from some of the tribes under the encouragement of the British.

With the signing of the Treaty of Greenville, peace came to the Allegheny Valley and  white settlers moved in to prosper from the riches of the Valley. At first there were farmers who came to take advantage of the free land and to travel the Allegheny to points west. Following them small settlements were built and trade and commerce began to develop along the Allegheny. In time transportation improved from canoes, flat boats and keel boats to steamboats with the capability to travel from Olean to Pittsburgh and beyond.

## Along the Allegheny

Pittsburgh became a major center for building steam engines for the western rivers. The Allegheny River and French creek connection to the Great Lakes, as well as its direct link to the Ohio River and points west, became the main attraction for the development of Pennsylvania Mainline Canal and its western divisions. As the years went by the Allegheny River came to be the modern river system we know today, complete with locks and dams, flood control dams, and heavily used for commercial and recreational purposes. If the Allegheny could speak, it would tell us many tales of tragedy, excitement, and jubilation.

# References


[1] Kent, Barry C. (1994). <u>Discovering Pennsylvania's Archeological Heritage</u> pp. 24-25. Pennsylvania Historical and Museum Commission.

[2] Kent, Barry C. (1994). <u>Discovering Pennsylvania's Archeological Heritage</u> pp. 26-27. Pennsylvania Historical and Museum Commission.

[3] Reader's Digest Association. (October 1984). <u>America's Fascinating Indian Heritage</u> pp. 34-35

[4] Dragoo, Don W. (1963). <u>Mounds for the Dead</u>. p. 137. Carnegie Museum.

[5] Everts, L. H. (1879). <u>History of Cattaraugas County, New York</u>. pp. 11-12. Press J. P. Lippencolt.

[6] Mayer-Oakes, William J. (1955). <u>Prehistory of the Upper Ohio Valley</u>. pp. 7-10 Carnegie Museum.

[7] Myer, Andrew J., Appalachean Archeological Consultants. (April 17th,1998). <u>An Overview of the McFate Culture of Northwestern Pennsylvania: The Last Prehistoric Inhabitants of Elk County.</u>

[8] Kussart, Serepta. (1938). <u>The Allegheny River</u> p.1. Burgum Printing Company, Pittsburgh, PA.

[9] Sipe, C. Hale (1927). <u>Indian Chiefs of Pennsylvania</u> pp. 14-15. The Zeigler Printing Company.

[10] Sipe, C. Hale (1927). <u>Indian Chiefs of Pennsylvania</u> pp.

19-20. The Zeigler Printing Company.

[11] Sherrow, Victorio (1992). <u>The Iroquois Indians</u> pp. 13-21. Chelsea House Publishers.

[12] Wallace, Paul A. W.(1993). <u>Indians in Pennsylvania</u> pp. 94-95 second edition.Commonwealth of Pennsylvania, the Pennsylvania Historical and Museum Commission.

[13] Sipe, C. Hale (1927). <u>Indian Chiefs of Pennsylvania</u>. p. 24. The Zeigler Printing Company.

[14] Schenck, J. S. & Rann, W. S. (1887). <u>History of Warren County</u>. D. Mason and Company Publishing.

[15] Editors of Time-Life Books. (1992). <u>The Euroupean Challenge</u> pp. 75-76.

[16] Sipe, C. Hale (1927). <u>The Indian Chiefs of Pennsylvania</u> p. 22. The Zeigler Printing Company.

[17] Chapman, T. J. (1887). <u>The French in the Allegheny</u> pp. 9-22. W.W. Williams Publishers.

[18] Chapman, T. J. (1887). <u>The French in the Allegheny</u> pp. 9-22. W.W. Williams Publishers.

[19] Rupp, I. D. (1846). <u>Early History of Western Pennsylvania Appendix NO. VI. Washingtons Journal 1753</u>. Harrisburgh, PA, Reprinted by Wennawoods Publishing 1995.

[20] Downes, Randolph C. (1940). <u>Council of Fires on the Upper Ohio</u> p. 68. The University of Pittsburgh Press

[21] Sipe, C. Hale (1927). <u>Indian Chiefs of Pennsylvania</u> pp.

249-250, The Zeigler Printing Company.

22  Rupp, I. D. (1846). <u>Early History of Western Pennsylvania</u>, pp. 121-129. reprinted by Wennawood Publishing, 1995

23  Baldwin, Leland (1937). <u>Pittsburgh, The Story of a City</u> pp. 48-52. University of Pittsburgh

24  Rupp, I. D. (1846). <u>Early History of Western Pennsylvania, Frederick Posts Second Journal</u>. pp. 118 and 120. Harrisburg Pa., reprinted by Wennawoods Publishing, 1995.

25  Lorant, Stefan (1988).  <u>Pittsburgh, The Story of an American City, fourth edition</u> p. 38. Authors Edition Inc.

26  Lorant, Stefan (1988).  <u>Pittsburgh, The Story of an American City, fourth edition</u> p. 38. Authors Edition Inc.

27  Parkman, Francis.(1851) <u>The Conspiracy of Pontiac</u> (6th rev. ed.) pp. 553-557. Little Brown and Company, reprinted by The Library of America, 1991.

28  Parkman, Francis. (1851). <u>The Conspiracy of Pontiac</u> (6th rev. ed.) pp. 632-634. Little Brown and Company, reprinted by The Library of America, 1991.

29  Parkman, Francis. (1851). <u>The Conspiracy of Pontiac</u> (6th rev. ed.) pp. 634-635. Little Brown and Company, reprinted by The Library of America, 1991.

30  Eaton, S. J. M. & Bell, Herbert. (1976) <u>History of Venango County</u> pp. 57-58. Brown, Runk and Company Pub-

lisher.

31  Rupp, I. D. (1846). <u>Early History of Western Pennsyl-vania</u> p. 154. Harrisburg Pa., reprinted by Wennawoods Publishing 1995.

32  Sipe, C. Hale 1931. <u>The Indian Wars of Pennsylvania</u> (second edition) pp. 424-425. The Telegraph Press

33  Stotz, Charles M. (1985). <u>Outposts of the War for the Empire.</u> II 65, 1978. Historical Society of Western Pennsyl-vania.  University of Pittsburgh Press

34  Harpster, John W (1938). <u>Pen Pictures of Early Western Pennsylvania: Journal of William Trent</u> pp. 103-104. Uni-versity of Pittsburgh Press

35  Parkman, Francis. (1851). <u>The Conspiracy of Pontiac</u> (6th rev. ed.) pp. 636-637. Little Brown and Company, re-printed by The Library of America, 1991.

36  Parkman, Francis. (1851). <u>The Conspiracy of Pontiac</u> (6th rev. ed.) p. 637.  Little Brown and Company, reprinted by The Library of America, 1991.

37  Sipe, C. Hale (1927). <u>Indian Chiefs of Pennsylvania</u> p. 399. The Zeigler Printing Company.

38  Rupp, I. D. (1846). <u>Early History of Western Pennsyl-vania</u> p. 179. Harrisburg, Pa., reprinted by Wennawoods Publishing,1995.

39  Wallace, Paul A. W. (1962). <u>Pennsylvania Seed of a Nation</u> p. 99. Harper and Row Publishers, NY and Evan-ston.

[40] Heckewelder, John (1818). History, Manners, and Customs of The Indian Nations pp. 342-343. Arno Press and New York times, reprinted 1971

[41] Downes, Randolph C. (1940). Council of Fires on the Upper Ohio p. 250. University of Pittsburgh Press.

[42] Fischer, Joseph R. (1997). A Well Executed Failure p. 115. University of South Carolina Press.

[43] Downes, Randolph C. (1940). Council of Fires on the Upper Ohio. p. 251. University of Pittsburgh Press.

[44] Fischer, Joseph R. (1997). A well Executed Failure p. 114. University of South Carolina Press.

[45] Pennsylvania Archives. 1779. Vol 7.

[46] Pennsylvania Archives. 1779. Vol 7.

[47] Downes, Randolph C. (1968). Council of Fires on the Upper Ohio p. 252. University of Pittsburgh Press.

[48] Fischer, Joseph R. (1997). A Well Executed Failure p. 115. University of South Carolina Press.

[49] DeMay, John A.(1997). The Settlers Forts of Western Pennsylvania p. 69. Clossen Press.

[50] Sipe, C. Hale The Indian Chiefs of Pennsylvania p. 517. Wennawwods Publishing

[51] Eckert, Allan W. (1995). That Dark and Bloody River p. 310. Bantam Books.

[52] Downs, Randolph C. (1940). <u>Council Fires on the Upper Ohio</u> pp. 291-292. University of Pittsburgh Press.

[53] Waterman, Watkins, and Co.(1895). <u>History of Butler County</u>. pp. 17-22. Wallsworth Publishing Co.

[54] Smith, Robert W. (1883). <u>History of Armstrong County</u> p. 28. Waterman, Watkins and Company.

[55] USACOE (1974). <u>Flood Plain Information Allegheny River</u>

[56] Bartoli, F. (1796). <u>Ki-on-twog-ky, the Seneca Chief known as Cornplanter (ca. 1732-1836)</u>, Reprinted with the permission of the New York State Historical Society

[57] USACOE. (1974). <u>Allegheny River Navigation System, Vol. 1.</u>

[58] Marrin, Albert (1987). <u>Struggle for a Continent: The French and Indian Wars, 1690 to 1760</u> p. 32. Athenneum

[59] USACOE (1974). <u>Flood Plain Information Allegheny River</u>

[60] Everts, L. H. (1879). <u>History of Cattaraugas County, New York</u>. pp. 34-35. Press J. P. Lipencolt.

[61] USACOE (1974). <u>Allegheny River Navigation System</u>. Vol. 1

[62] Kussart, Serepta. (1938). <u>The Allegheny River</u> p. 47. Bergham Printing Company

[63] Day, Sherman (1843). <u>Historical Collections of</u>

Pennsylvania p. 182.

[64] Rosenberg, Max (1974). <u>The Building of Perry's Fleet on Lake Erie</u> pp. 11-20. Pennsylvania Historical and Museum Commission

[65] Kussart, S. (1938). <u>The Allegheny River</u> p. 58. Bergham Printing Company

[66] Kussart, S. (1938). <u>The Allegheny River</u> pp. 136-137. Bergham Printing Company

[67] Kussart, S. (1938). <u>The Allegheny River</u> pp. 137-138. Bergham Printing Company

[68] Kussart, S. (1938). <u>The Allegheny River</u> pp. 138-139. Bergham Printing Company

[69] Way, Frederick, Jr. (1942). <u>The Allegheny</u> pp. 225-270. Farrar and Rinehart Inc.

[70] Shank, William H. (1981). <u>The Amazing Pennsylvania Canals</u>, Sixth Anniversary Edition, pp. 19-21. American Canal and Transportation Center, York, PA.

[71] Shank, William H. (1981). <u>The Amazing Pennsylvania Canals</u>, Sixth Anniversary Edition, pp. 19-20. American Canal and Transportation Center, York, PA.

[72] Shank, William H. (1981). <u>The Amazing Pennsylvania Canals</u>, Sixth Anniversary Edition, p. 20. American Canal and Transportation Center, York, PA.

[73] Shank, William H. (1981). <u>The Amazing Pennsylvania Canals</u>, Sixth Anniversary Edition, pp. 21-22. American

Canal and Transportation Center, York, PA..

[74] Shank, William H. (1981). <u>The Amazing Pennsylvania Canals</u>, Sixth Anniversary Edition, p. 55. American Canal and Transportation Center, York, PA.

[75] Shank, William H. (1981). <u>The Amazing Pennsylvania Canals</u>, Sixth Anniversary Edition, p. 56. American Canal and Transportation Center, York, PA.

[76] Shank, William H. (1981). <u>The Amazing Pennsylvania Canals</u>, Sixth Anniversary Edition, p. 56. American Canal and Transportation Center, York, PA.

[77] Shank, William H. (1981). <u>The Amazing Pennsylvania Canals</u>, Sixth Anniversary Edition, p. 56. American Canal and Transportation Center, York, PA.

# Index

# Index